Walking in the dark

Manchester University Press

For Patricia, Leona, Miranda and Annabel, who have been there at every step, providing light and love when he shuffled into the unknown.

Walking in the dark

James Baldwin, my father, and me

Douglas Field

Manchester University Press

Published by Manchester University Press
Oxford Road, Manchester, M13 9PL

www.manchesteruniversitypress.co.uk

British Library Cataloguing-in-Publication Data
A catalogue record for this book is available from the British Library

ISBN 978 1 5261 7517 5 hardback

First published 2024

Typeset in Freight
by R. J. Footring Ltd, Derby, UK

You're always in difficulty with a book.

James Baldwin, 'It's Hard To Be James Baldwin' (1972)

Contents

Contents

Prologue

If we are not ourselves, who are we?

Most of us, no matter what we say, are walking in the dark, whistling in the dark. Nobody knows what is going to happen to him from one moment to the next, or how one will bear it.

James Baldwin, interview with Studs Terkel (1961)

I wish I'd been there but, as usual, I wasn't.

My father, Richard Field, was not a patient man. But in November 2022, he spent several hours watching his neighbour, Doris, piece together a jigsaw puzzle with the calmness of a heron waiting for its supper. I'm not sure what type of puzzle Doris was completing, but after nearly three hours she held the final piece between her thumb and forefinger, smiling as she sensed victory. My father, who had not spoken a word during the last few hours, and who had barely moved, leapt out of his chair with the agility of a five-year-old. He swiped the final puzzle piece from Doris's trembling hand and popped it into his mouth. I like to think he grinned as he swallowed the final piece.

The previous time I'd seen my father, he had barely spoken at all. He had recently moved into a care home in north Shropshire, initially just for respite, after Alzheimer's disease started colonising his mind. I'd arrived at his new residence with one of my younger sisters. We tried to coax our father into conversation and recognition, but he sat in a wingback chair, hunched and sunken, tugging at his unkempt beard with such force that he yanked out clumps. (I winced, but he did not.) We took our father outside, hoping that the fresh air might stimulate him. He turned to my sister and pointed at the pot of buddleias outside the home. 'Patso', he said, mistaking his daughter for his wife, 'look at the poems'.

I have no idea whether my father mistook flowers for poems or whether there was something poetic he saw in that moment. But as I have learned with my father, Alzheimer's snuffs out narrative; comments are no longer threaded together into conversations but, instead, are merely a stop-start series of utterances, often bearing no relation to each other. Start. Stop. Begin again. When I spend time with my father, I realise that I am seeking how to gather his scattered comments into a narrative I can understand. Flowers become poems, I hope, because there's a part of my father still there, whose passion for the poetry of Thomas Hardy, Philip Larkin, John Betjeman and Dylan Thomas was matched only by his delight in spending time with people. Until a few years ago, my father could recite long poems and sections of plays by heart. My older sister's middle name is Cordelia because of my father's love of *King Lear*. Now, when his three daughters profess their love, there is little or no recognition. 'I fear I am not in my perfect mind', Lear tells Cordelia, a line that my father would have delighted in using, had his memory allowed. In the early stages of his illness, he pinned to the wall of his flat a coaster which read, 'I have lost my mind and I am making no effort to look for it'.

I left the care home as my father sank back into a chair, his fingers fidgeting as he slept, hunched to one side.

Prologue

Georges Perec's masterpiece *Life: A User's Manual* begins with a preamble about jigsaw puzzles. For Perec, who spent a career making and solving enigmas of one kind and another, puzzles were a way of making sense of the world, a way of understanding how life, often seemingly unfathomable, is, in fact, a series of intricate puzzles that can be pieced together. Perec – who once wrote (in French) an entire novel without using the letter 'e' – explained the art of puzzles as follows:

> the parts do not determine the pattern, but the pattern de-
> termines the parts.... The only thing that counts is the ability
> to link this piece to other pieces, and in that sense the art
> of the jigsaw puzzle has something in common with the art
> of go. The pieces are readable, take on a sense, only when
> assembled; in isolation, a puzzle piece means nothing – just
> an impossible question, an opaque challenge.[1]

As I have been trying to make sense of my father's illness, I have thought often about puzzles. There are missing pieces in the network of my father's brain: recognition, nostalgia and contemplation no longer seem to function; his brain is suffocating with a disease that will not allow connections to be made. There are also missing pieces of information as I have tried to thread my father's life together. He has one cousin, whom I have never met, and no siblings to fill in the gaps about his life. I could not write a biography of my father since there are so many details that drift, like seaweed, pulled by currents and then washed ashore. As I think about my father, I am reminded that we are creatures of narrative; as Joan Didion tells us, we impose stories on 'the shifting phantasmagoria which is our actual experience'.[2] Biographers pull strands of detail together to make sense of lives, but, in so doing, they often cover over gaps in their subject's life history, skating over moments of uncertainty. In my father's case, the past is mixed up with the present and his future has become relentlessly familiar. He drifts around the care home today as he will drift around it tomorrow, his shipwrecked memories scattered, hidden and lost.

~~~~~

I feel nervous as I ring the bell at the care home. It is the time of the COVID-19 pandemic, and on entry I wash my hands, sign in and mask up my face, something that will surely confuse my father further. A year ago, he would have chuckled at the poster of a First World War soldier in the lobby, with the caption 'Lest We Forget', in a home where most of the residents suffer from varying forms of dementia. ('We are the Dead', wrote John McCrae in 'In Flanders Fields'. 'Short days ago / We lived ... '.)[3] Sometimes he is asleep when I visit, his thin body bent double in the chair. I look out for Doris and wonder if she is wary of my father. I search for clues that my father is still there; I believe, for a while at least, that his charisma and vitality will pierce through the protein that suffocates his brain. On a recent visit to my father's care home, I find myself disorientated, as he has changed rooms. He is asleep on his bed, with his mouth open and slightly twisted so that even in slumber he does not seem at peace with his world. His nose looks as though it has been broken, which might have happened during one of his customary falls, and his teeth now resemble date stones, but his skin, even at the age of eighty, is smooth and supple. I look around his room and notice that our surname, which is stuck on laminated paper to his half-opened door, has been changed from Field to Fields. It is the kind of detail – errant apostrophes and letters out of place – that he once would have noticed in a flash. For a moment, reading 'Richard Fields' increases my feeling of estrangement from my father, but then I think about striking out his first name and replacing it with 'Strawberry', or 'Elysian', the kind of mischievous caper he would have enjoyed. 'What's in a name?', I wonder; that which we call a flower sounds as sweet as a poem.

~~~~~

Jigsaw-gate, as it became known in our family, gave us a rare moment of cheer in a clouded period as my father's condition deteriorated. In December, he pushed over the home's Christmas tree, telling staff, 'I don't like the decorations' – a further glimpse, or so I hoped, that his passion and fire had not been fully snuffed out. The puzzles I've been trying to resolve are interlocking. At times, I wonder whether my father can connect the pieces of his memory together, or whether my infrequent visits are for his or my benefit. None of this quite makes sense, like mourning for someone still living, which is something that my family and I must learn to do.

In *Life: A User's Manual*, Percival Bartlebooth, an eccentric British millionaire, decides one day to take up painting watercolours. He sets off round the world to paint 500 harbours and ports, which takes him twenty years. Every other week, he sends the paintings to his assistant, Gaspard Winckler, who mounts the watercolours onto a board and turns them into jigsaws, each with 750 pieces. Bartlebooth returns home to solve the difficult puzzles that Winckler has made. He is well on his way to completing the task he had set himself but is perplexed by one of the shapes:

It is the twenty-third of June nineteen seventy-five, and it is eight o'clock in the evening. Seated at his jigsaw puzzle, Bartlebooth has just died. On the tablecloth, somewhere in the crepuscular sky of the four hundred and thirty-ninth puzzle, the black hole of the sole piece not yet filled in has the almost perfect shape of an X. But the ironical thing, which could have been foreseen long ago, is that the piece the dead man holds between his fingers is shaped like a W.[4]

~~~~~

My father, an English teacher for forty years, was my foremost literary influence. I don't recall him telling me what I should read, but he encouraged me to browse the bookshelves in his study: books by Hermann Hesse and Martin Amis – I remember being disturbed by the title *Dead Babies* – and works by Carl Jung and George Gurdjieff, the latter an Armenian mystic and composer who urged his followers to rouse themselves from their 'waking sleep'. I pored over works by Reshad Feild, a name similar to my father's, whose books introduced me to Sufi mysticism, and I spent days reading the works of his favourite guru, Bhagwan Shree Rajneesh, also known as Osho, whose ninety-odd Rolls-Royce cars had confounded the West, where it was assumed that he must be a spiritual confidence man rather than a mystic. When Rajneesh moved to Oregon, my father told me, Americans were so dumbfounded by the sight of an Indian with a fleet of Rolls-Royces that when they stood gaping in amazement, he popped a bit of truth inside their mouths.

One of the few books that my father suggested I read was James Baldwin's first collection of essays, *Notes of a Native Son* – an old Corgi edition that he had thumbed since his undergraduate days. On the back cover, an intense and suave Baldwin wearing a sharp houndstooth suit compels and confronts the reader to tackle his book. My father told me that he had seen Baldwin at the University of Cambridge in 1965 during a Union debate with the conservative polemicist William F. Buckley Jr. Thirty years later, my father's recollection was poor in terms of detail, but he recalled Baldwin's voice and presence with excitement. 'When he spoke', my father explained, 'his presence pinned you to your chair. I had never heard such fierce eloquence'.

Voice played an important part in my family in telling truth from lies. It came from my father's mother, Peggy, whose brilliant mind became embittered with gin martinis, which fuelled her emotional attacks on my father, her only child. 'Listen to her voice', she told me, aged around five, as Margaret Thatcher came to power. 'You can tell she's lying by the tone of her voice. Never trust people who lie with their voices.'

In 'Autobiographical Notes', the first essay in *Notes of a Native Son*, Baldwin's voice refused to be tethered to the page. 'I love to argue with people who do not disagree with me too profoundly', the writer explained in his late twenties, 'and I love to laugh'. He ends the essay with what I used to think was a modest ambition: 'I want to be an honest man and a good writer' – qualities, I realise now, that are not easy to achieve.[5]

But if Baldwin wrote with a piercing clarity, a style of writing that seems effortless, then it was his refusal to shy away from complexity that later drew me in. The next essay in *Notes of a Native Son*, 'Everybody's Protest Novel', published when Baldwin was not yet in his mid-twenties, is written with the bravado of youth, as well as its wisdom. It is an essay in which Baldwin slew his own literary father of sorts,

Richard Wright, the most famous living African American writer, author of the bestselling novel *Native Son* (1940), a tour de force of late naturalism which tells the story of Bigger Thomas, a disillusioned young Black man living in a Chicago slum. Bigger is a product of his environment: he becomes the monster that white society has feared but has also created.

'Everybody's Protest Novel' is one of the most explosive early essays by an American writer.[6] Baldwin is merciless as he dismisses Harriet Beecher Stowe, author of *Uncle Tom's Cabin* – a celebrated novel long associated with the abolition of slavery – as merely a pamphleteer. *Uncle Tom's Cabin*, Baldwin tells us – as though he were flicking crumbs off his lapel – 'is a very bad novel' that wallows in sentimentality.[7] Wright, who has been waiting in the wings of this long essay, is then hauled onto Baldwin's stage. Bigger, Baldwin informs the reader – in a description that would have enraged his one-time mentor – 'is Uncle Tom's descendant, flesh of his flesh, so exactly opposite a portrait that, when the books are placed together, it seems that the contemporary Negro novelist and the dead New England woman are locked together in a deadly, timeless battle; the one uttering merciless exhortations, the other shouting curses'.[8]

Wright, a colossus of American literature, understandably felt betrayed by this upstart's dismissal of his most famous novel. Baldwin had followed him to Paris in 1948, and the essay marked the denouement of their friendship, a tipping point in which the ageing heavyweight boxer was embarrassed by the dancing uppercuts of the new kid on the block. Rereading 'Everybody's Protest Novel' after witnessing my father's illness – and in particular after jigsaw-gate – it was the following two sentences that grabbed me:

> Our passion for categorization, life neatly fitted into pegs, has led to an unforeseen, paradoxical distress; confusion, a

breakdown of meaning. Those categories which were meant to define and control the world for us have boomeranged us into chaos; in which limbo we whirl, clutching the straws of our definitions.[9]

Baldwin is discussing the limitations of protest fiction, but his suspicion of categories and labels – 'life neatly fitted into pegs' – or jigsaw pieces, has become something of a mantra for me as I walk through a world that seems ever-more pre-occupied with categories, divisions and simplicity, something which my father's illness has upended.

~~~~~

Teaching was a vocation, rather than simply a job, for my father, who believed in literature as a means of understanding people and the world around us, a view that he shared with Baldwin. 'You think your pain and your heartbreak are unprecedented in the history of the world', the writer explained, 'but then you read. It was books that taught me that the things that tormented me most were the very things that connected me with all the people who were alive, who had ever been alive.'[10] 'You don't need to study sociology', my father told me when I had expressed an interest in the subject, 'just read literature to understand how people work'. It was a view that reminded me of Baldwin's statement, early in his career, that 'literature and sociology are not one and the same; it is impossible to discuss them as if they were'.[11] My father was an astute close reader, who found moments of tenderness in Alexander Pope's armour-plated iambic pentameter, and he homed in on the spirituality of poets such as T. S. Eliot, as well as finding moments of warmth in the usually cool Philip Larkin. Reading was central to his life, a solitary pursuit that connected him to the world around him.

My father spent much of his free time with students who were struggling with the literature he was teaching. When one of his pupils told him that he did not like poetry, my father explained that this was like saying that he did not like music; that there were so many different styles and genres of poetry, that it was just a case of finding the right sound. He could also be fierce when he thought that his students were not taking their studies seriously, or if they failed to be moved by literature that touched his soul. I don't remember my father crying, but music and literature could make him 'prickly behind the eyes', as he called it. A friend who was taught by my father recalled how the class were still talking loudly when he entered the room. He picked up a chair and threw it against the wall, which stunned the class into silence.

Although Baldwin is best known as a writer and activist, he was an astute observer of the US education system, and he became a university lecturer late in life. The importance of education is a theme that threads through his writing and talks, particularly the damaging effects of white power and history on young Black children. Between September and October 1957, Baldwin travelled extensively in the American South, to cities including Charlotte, North Carolina, Atlanta, Georgia, and Little Rock, Arkansas. During his hectic schedule, he met Martin Luther King Jr., his wife Coretta, and the noted folklorist Sterling Brown, as well as teachers and students. In 'A Fly in Buttermilk', written three years after the Supreme Court ruled that 'separate educational facilities are inherently unequal' in 1954, and less than a year after the Montgomery Bus Boycott, Baldwin bore witness to the damaging effects of schools in the South, where segregation remained firmly in place. 'The teachers have themselves arrived at a dead end',

Baldwin observed, 'for in a segregated school system they cannot rise any higher, and the students are aware of this. Both students and teachers soon cease to struggle'.[12]

Baldwin was also keenly attuned to the importance of what African American students should be taught. On 16 October 1963, he gave a talk titled 'The Negro Child – His Self Image', which was published as 'A Talk to Teachers', which he begins by reminding his readers that 'we are living through a very dangerous time', a statement born out of the tumultuous events of that year. On 12 June, Medgar Evers, a prominent Civil Rights activist, whom Baldwin knew, was assassinated outside his Mississippi home by a white supremacist. A few months later, on 15 September, four girls – Addie Mae Collins, Carol Denise McNair, Carole Robertson and Cynthia Wesley – were murdered by members of the Ku Klux Klan when they bombed a Baptist church in Alabama. Two boys, Johnny Robinson and Virgil Ware, were killed in the aftermath of the bombing. Two months later, President John F. Kennedy was assassinated in Dallas, Texas. Amid the political turmoil of the early 1960s, Baldwin reminds his readers that 'It is almost impossible for any Negro child to discover anything about his actual history'.[13] Each Black child, Baldwin points out, is 'born in the shadow of the stars and stripes' but is 'also assured by his country and his countrymen that he has never contributed anything to civilization – that his past is nothing more than a record of humiliations gladly endured'.[14]

Education, for Baldwin, is closely linked to the word's Latin root, *educare*, meaning to lead out or bring forth. Education, in other words, should equip students with the knowledge to question the ways that culture, including education itself, is never arbitrary or neutral; rather, it is always a reflection of those who seek to maintain power. Or, as Baldwin puts it, 'one of the paradoxes of education' is 'that precisely at the point when you begin to develop a conscience, you must find yourself at war with your society'.[15] And while Baldwin, a *soi-disant* 'disturber of the peace', championed iconoclasm, he was nonetheless aware that 'What societies really, ideally, want is a citizenry which will simply obey the rules of society'.[16]

During his childhood, Baldwin's most inspirational teachers encouraged him to question the rules of society and to read and think critically about the world around him. When he was five years old, he started school at P.S. 24 in Harlem in 1929, the year of the stock market crash, where his head teacher, Gertrude E. Ayer, was the first Black principal in New York City. At Frederick Douglass Junior High, in need of guidance and support that were not forthcoming from his father, Baldwin was encouraged to write by Herman W. Porter, a Black graduate of Harvard, who made Baldwin editor-in-chief of *The Douglass Pilot*, the school magazine. Baldwin was also taught by Countee Cullen, a leading poet of the Harlem Renaissance – also known as the New Negro Movement, an unprecedented cultural and intellectual flowering of Black creative expression that was focused in Manhattan, but which spread to northern cities including Chicago – whose sojourns in France inspired his student to follow in his footsteps. But it was Orilla 'Bill' Miller, a young white Midwestern teacher, who made a lasting impression on the aspiring writer, to the extent that he 'never really managed to hate white people'.[17] Bonding over a shared love of Dickens, Miller took the budding writer to the theatre and to the cinema, which Baldwin recalled as pivotal moments in his development as a writer in his book-length essay about film, *The Devil Finds Work* (1976). Along with Miller, the painter Beauford Delaney played an instrumental role in Baldwin's development as an artist, by teaching him how to see the world around him, and how to hear it, whether it was the sublime wonder of oil refracted in a dank city puddle, or the jagged lyricism of the blues that his father forbade him to hear.

Baldwin gave talks at numerous universities during his career, but he did not join a faculty until he was invited to become a lecturer at Bowling Green University, Ohio, in 1978, to which he returned a few years later; Baldwin also taught at various times at the University of California, Berkeley, and at the University of Massachusetts Amherst. Baldwin's approach to teaching, like my father's, was focused on getting students engaged and passionate about literature. Achieving high marks was important, but only if teaching achieved other goals, such as liberating students from the tyranny of conventional thinking. In 'Sonny's Blues', Baldwin's most frequently anthologised short story, first published in 1957, the narrator is an algebra teacher whose successful career based on empirical knowledge is contrasted with that of his brother, the eponymous Sonny, a troubled jazz musician and heroin addict. During the course of the story, in which the narrator watches his brother play at a jazz club, he learns from Sonny, who, despite his wayward ways, including his addiction and arrest, understands how to transform his suffering through his music.

Baldwin was not a conventional university lecturer who prepared classes and adhered to institutional rules. As a child preacher, he had learned to extemporise, delivering sermons as the spirit took him, a skill that prepared him for teaching. One of his colleagues from the University of Massachusetts recollects that Baldwin 'simply spoke about what was striking him at that specific moment'.[18] He stayed up late drinking whisky and discussing literature and politics with his colleagues and slept through early-morning seminars. Colleagues affectionately referred to his erratic timekeeping as 'Jimmy time'. But he was also generous with his time, especially when it came to his students. The writer Ekwueme Michael Thelwell recalls how he would meet with every student who waited to see him during his office hours, however long it took.[19]

Much like my father, Baldwin was driven by a desire to lead his students towards a kind of *satori* in which they opened their eyes, not only to the craft of the texts they studied, but also to the society which produced them. At Bowling Green, he taught novels and short stories by William Faulkner, Philip Roth and Harriet Beecher Stowe, but his classes, as one of his biographers puts it, 'quickly became forums for larger questions of identity. What did it mean to be "white" or to think one was "white" or "black"?'[20] From his accounts of teaching at university, it is clear that Baldwin valued the time he spent with his students; that he viewed teaching as an opportunity to learn from his students, rather than simply imparting his knowledge to them. 'The irreducible price of learning is realizing that you do not know', Baldwin wrote in 1980.[21]

By the time Baldwin started lecturing at universities in the late 1970s, his career was waning, to the point that he was in danger of being forgotten outside of the academy, or 'unremembered', as his old teacher Countee Cullen put it in 'Heritage', one of his most famous poems. 'In the process of memory undone', as one scholar puts it, reflecting on his diminishing reputation after his death, but before his current renaissance, 'Baldwin is not just forgotten; he is made unknown: less read, cited, anthologized, argued over, taught, and thought about than he used to be'.[22] Although his career started before the Civil Rights Movement, it was during the 1960s that Baldwin became a national, and then global, phenomenon. And it's worth remembering that he was one of the only major African American writers who participated in the movement as both an author and activist. Richard Wright died in 1960, while Ralph Ellison, one of the most talented American writers of the last century, believed that engaging with politics diluted a writer's craft. And Lorraine Hansberry, whom Baldwin greatly admired, used the success of her play *A Raisin in the Sun* (which opened in 1959) to become a prominent voice in the struggle for Black liberation until her death, aged only thirty-four, from cancer. By the late 1970s, when Baldwin started lecturing – a decade after Martin Luther King Jr. was assassinated, and as neoliberalism started to infect the globe – the community-driven activism of the Civil Rights Movement and Black Power Movement seemed like an age away.

During the mid-1980s, as the United States stewed in an unsavoury dish of neoliberalism and conservativism, debates were waged over the meaning of America: what the nation was and what it would become. While issues such as gun control, abortion and same-sex marriage were fiercely contested, schools were a central battleground since they were seen as the institutions most likely to reproduce the status quo through an ideologically skewed national curriculum. Not surprisingly, then, in the mid-1980s Toni Morrison told an interviewer that reclaiming African American history was 'paramount in its importance' during a period of wilful forgetfulness about America's role in enslavement.[23] In her novels such as *Beloved* and *Sula*, the past, often connected to the trauma of slavery, is unbearably painful, but as Morrison implores, it must be dredged up and confronted.

Baldwin's writing is a reminder that history and the past are not the same thing. 'It is a sentimental error', he warns, 'to believe that the past is dead; it means nothing to say that it is all forgotten, that the Negro himself has forgotten it', and he points out that 'It is not a question of memory'.[24] For while the trauma of the whip and chain may no longer be in living memory, the past is always calling out to the present. In much of his non-fiction, Baldwin warns readers of what he called 'the trap of history'. In his essay 'The White Man's Guilt', published in August 1965 – six months after the assassination of Malcolm X – Baldwin explains that 'History, as nearly no one seems to know, is not merely something to be read. And it does not refer merely, or even principally, to the past. On the contrary, the great force of history comes from the fact that we carry it within us.'[25] Time and time again, Baldwin reminds us that until 'innocent' white America faces up to its past, 'people have no other hope. They are ... still trapped in a history which they do not understand.'[26] Or as he put it succinctly in his masterful essay 'Stranger in the Village', 'people are trapped in history and history is trapped in them'.[27]

Baldwin's death in 1987 coincided with the publication of Morrison's *Beloved*, a work that explores the effects of trauma, memory and repression, themes that resonate across both writers' work. In Morrison's novel, which was based on the true story of Margaret Garner, Sethe escapes with her young children from a brutal slavery plantation. When she is caught, she kills her daughter rather than consign her to the horrors of slavery. By the time the slave patrol finds Sethe, she is living as a free woman, but she is trapped by her past. She begins each day with 'the serious work of beating back the past', while beginning to understand the need to confront it.[28] But when the past returns in the embodied form of her dead daughter, the eponymous Beloved, Sethe is released from the burden of repressing her past, but she is also unable to stop remembering, a process that almost destroys her.

His last book, *The Evidence of Things Not Seen* (1985), is a long essay about the Atlanta child murders that took place between 1979 and 1981, published two years before *Beloved* – a novel in which, as Morrison explained, 'Nobody ... can bear too long to dwell on the past; nobody can avoid it'.[29] Baldwin begins with a meditation on memory and writes: 'no one wishes to be plunged, head down, in the torrent of what he does not remember and does not wish to remember'. But as he also makes clear, what is forgotten, or 'misremembered' as Morrison calls it, 'controls the human being. What one does not remember dictates who one loves or fails to love', and he adds 'What one does not remember is the serpent in the garden of one's dreams'.[30]

History is viewed with suspicion by both Morrison and Baldwin. 'People who imagine that history flatters them (as it does, indeed, since they wrote it)', Baldwin wrote, 'are impaled on their history like a butterfly on a pin and become incapable of seeing or changing themselves, or the world'.[31] And like Morrison, who explained in an essay on *Beloved* that it was paramount to 'substitute and rely on memory rather than history because I knew I could not, should not, trust recorded history', Baldwin calls attention to the importance of the past, rather than history.[32]

Baldwin did not write an autobiography, but he frequently invoked his own experiences in his essays to explain the world around him. *No Name in the Street*, a book-length essay that was first published in 1972, is perhaps the closest thing in print we have to Baldwin's extended reflections on his life, written during the tumultuous period between 1967 and 1971, which included a prolonged bout of despair brought on after the murder Martin Luther King Jr. in 1968. In it, Baldwin recalls his journey from writer to activist. In one of the more reflective sections of this long essay, he muses

how 'Time passes and passes. It passes backwards and it
passes forward and it carries you along.' And while time
'is carrying you through an element you do not understand
into an element you will not remember', Baldwin posits that
nonetheless '*something* remembers – it can even be said that
something avenges'.[33]

Notwithstanding his philosophical meditations on
memory, *No Name in the Street* is marked by an example of
Baldwin misremembering an important historical event. In
1956, as he recalls, he was covering the first International
Congress of Black Writers and Artists at the Sorbonne in
Paris, where he was living. The congress, which ran from 19
to 22 September, was a historic moment in which intellectuals of African descent gathered to discuss the abolition of
racism and colonialism. Organised by the Senegalese writer
and activist Alioune Diop, who had founded the influential
journal *Présence Africaine* nearly a decade earlier, the congress
bustled with intellectuals from the African diaspora, among
them Richard Wright and the Martinican poet and playwright
Aimé Césaire. Missing from the proceedings, however, was
W. E. B. Du Bois, the author of *The Souls of Black Folk* (1903),
a leading figure in African American literature and culture,
whose passport had been withheld by the US government.

Baldwin recalls how 'one bright afternoon', he and fellow
writers 'were meandering up the Boulevard St-Germain, on
the way to lunch'. The leisurely stroll, Baldwin recounts,
was ruptured by the photograph of an African American
student 'on every newspaper kiosk'. It showed a dignified
teenager, Dorothy Counts, who was, at the time, the only
Black student to enrol at the recently desegregated Harry
Harding High School in Charlotte, North Carolina. Douglas
Martin's famous photograph of Counts walking to school
won World Press Photograph of the Year, but Baldwin could

also have seen pictures taken by Don Sturkey, which show an animated white mob jeering at a resolute – and no doubt terrified – student trying to get to school. The image of a Black student who was 'reviled and spat upon by the mob' of several hundred white people as she made her way to school had a profound effect on Baldwin. It convinced him that he 'could ... no longer sit around in Paris discussing the Algerian and the black American problem. Everybody else was paying their dues, and it was time I went home and paid mine'.[34]

Baldwin indeed returned to America, where he became deeply involved in the Civil Rights Movement as a writer and activist, but his recollection of being compelled to leave France after seeing pictures of Dorothy Counts in 1956 is not possible since she did not start Harry Harding High School until September of the following year. Baldwin's first account of the congress, an acerbic essay called 'Princes and Powers', published in 1957, describes a very different scene from his recollections in *No Name in the Street*. In the earlier essay, the 'newspaper vendors seemed cheerful; so did the people who bought the newspapers'.[35] In *No Name in the Street*, Baldwin recalls how he was 'meandering' in Paris, how he had 'dawdled' in Europe – descriptions which are sharply contrasted with the urgency of the Civil Rights Movement.[36] During his trips to the US South, Baldwin recalls how he was marching 'wearily, marching, marching' along with Martin Luther King Jr., a reminder to readers of *No Name in the Street* that he had not lost his way as a writer and activist.[37]

In *No Name in the Street*, Baldwin recalls an early memory about his mother but acknowledges that 'much has been blotted out, coming back only lately in bewildering and un-trustworthy flashes'.[38] The mis-memory of Counts, however, seems something different. Written before he was fifty – at around the age I am now – the slippage may have something to do with the plasticity of memory. Some critics read this moment as the blindsiding effect of trauma in the writer's life, including a suicide attempt the year before. As the writer and academic Eddie Glaude Jr. reads it, the mistake reveals 'how trauma colored his witness. Memories fragmented or were repressed. Painful moments were triggered by random encounters. Grief and loss often overwhelmed everything.'[39] As Baldwin writes in the epilogue to *No Name in the Street*, 'This book has been much delayed by trials, assassinations, funerals, and despair'. And as he wrote in his last book, 'What I remembered – or imagined myself to remember – of my life in America (before I left home!) was terror.... Terror cannot be remembered.'[40]

Baldwin's slippage is reminiscent of a moment in *Patrimony* (1991), Philip Roth's memoir about his father, Herman. Roth, who frequently pushed the boundaries between fiction and autobiography – signalled by the book's subtitle, *A True Story* – recalls taking a wrong turn on the way to see his ailing father. Roth finds himself unexpectedly on the road to the cemetery, a slippage of sorts that he describes as 'narratively right', just as Baldwin's false recollection of seeing pictures of Counts made perfect narrative sense as a reason to compel him to join up with the burgeoning Civil Rights Movement.[41]

In my father's case, and that of many other sufferers of dementia, the illness, however, is brutally prosaic and bereft of any narrative beyond that of declension. The banality of Alzheimer's, a disease which creeps slowly over the brain, destroys not only its victims: like a bullet designed to incapacitate its target, it also takes down close friends and family. At present there is no cure for Alzheimer's, which is the most common type of dementia. An estimated 900,000 people in the UK are living with dementia, a figure that is likely rise to 1.4 million by 2040. In the United States, there are nearly 7 million people living specifically with Alzheimer's. Unless a cure is found, there may be as many as 12.7 million Americans living with the disease by 2050.[42] Women are more likely than men to develop dementia, and they are also more likely to end up as carers, while non-whites are disproportionally affected. It is also a peculiarly human disease. Long-living animals, among them whales and dolphins, may suffer from cognitive decline, but in a cruel twist only the animals seemingly most aware of their mortality are punished with the slow erosion of their cognitive abilities.

Paradoxically, dementia is both an ancient and a modern condition. For thousands of years, famous philosophers, among them Hippocrates, Plato and Pythagoras, believed that senile dementia was an inevitable part of ageing, rather than a disease. In *As You Like It*, 'melancholy Jaques' delivers one of Shakespeare's best-known speeches, in which 'one man in his time plays many parts'. The 'Last scene of all' 'Is second childishness and mere oblivion,/Sans teeth, sans eyes, sans taste, sans everything'. It was not until the end of the eighteenth century, when Philippe Pinel, dubbed 'the father of modern psychiatry', identified four types of mental disorder that dementia became a medical term, along with mania, melancholy and what was then called 'mental retardation'.[43]

It would take another hundred-odd years for Alois Alzheimer, a German psychiatrist and neuropathologist, to identify the first case of 'presenile dementia', which his colleague Emil Kraepelin termed 'Alzheimer's disease' in recognition of the discovery. In his first paper on the disease, which was published in 1907, Alzheimer recounts how a fifty-one-year-old woman, Auguste D. (Deter), had been admitted for psychiatric care in 1901, where she remained until her death nearly five years later. 'She is completely disoriented in time and space', Alzheimer explains. 'Her memory is seriously impaired.... Sometimes she says that she does not understand anything and that everything is strange to her'. Alzheimer describes how her condition deteriorated until, 'At the end, the patient was lying in bed in a fetal position completely pathetic, incontinent', a description that will be familiar to carers of those with dementia.[44]

The autopsy revealed that the cerebral cortex – the outer layer of the brain, which is responsible for memory, language and judgement – had atrophied to a point usually found in patients in their seventies. 'It looked like measles, or chicken pox, of the brain', the writer David Shenk explains. 'The cortex was specked with crusty brown plaques ... too many to count.'[45] The importance of the discovery notwithstanding, I find myself thinking less about the achievements of the German doctor but more about Auguste Deter, a wife, mother and sister, a well-educated seamstress from a working-class family in Frankfurt. During his examination of Auguste, Alzheimer asked his patient a series of questions, not unlike tests my father took several years ago, which determined her mental state. In response to the question 'Where are you right now?' Auguste replied, 'Here and everywhere, here and now, you must not think badly of me.' When she could no longer answer questions, exhausted and confused, she told Alzheimer, 'I have lost myself'.

As Susan Sontag pointed out in her 1989 book *AIDS and Its Metaphors*, there is nothing innocent about disease metaphors. She writes, 'The most terrifying illnesses are those perceived not just as lethal but as dehumanizing, literally so', a statement that captures the incorporeal language that surrounds Alzheimer's.[46] Unlike people with other illnesses, those living with Alzheimer's are frequently described as husks or ghosts of their former selves. Dementia sufferers are 'not themselves any longer'; during the long goodbye, they are 'the living dead' whose state of unbeing changes the perception of time not only for the sufferers but also for loved ones. 'My father used to love watching cricket' I find myself saying, a choice of tense that sits uncomfortably with me while my father is still alive. If, as Sontag proposes, 'cancer is not so much a disease of time as a disease or pathology of space', then the inverse may be said of those with Alzheimer's, who regress to adult infancy.[47] 'Retrogenesis' describes the correlation between the regression of people with Alzheimer's and the progression of child development. In the late stages of the disease, for example, which my father is approaching, skills such as smiling can be compared to the milestones of my four-month-old daughter.[48]

Retrogenesis may be one reason why there is so much discomfort around Alzheimer's, a disease which may creep up slowly on any of us, and which disturbs the comforting narrative of time. We might get a haircut or wear a new hat to break up the monotony of our sense of ourselves. We don't notice our hair growing, only when it needs to be cut, a way of glimpsing how others might perceive the changes that take place in our very being of which we are otherwise unaware. For my father, time seems to stand still; he is not even aware of his own reflection, and he takes no interest in what he is wearing, like my older daughter, who is two years old.

There is much more awareness of the disease now than there was among previous generations, so that those diagnosed in the early stages, like my father, must grapple with the concept of cognitive decline in real time as the brain loses momentum. And as Sontag explains, 'Any disease that is treated as a mystery and acutely feared enough will be felt to be morally, if not literally contagious'.[49] In the case of Alzheimer's, neurologists know what happens to the brain when the disease begins, but they do not know how to prevent or cure it. They know that the cerebral cortex eventually becomes choked with clumps of spherical plaques and stringy tangles. As the plaques and tangles spread, like weeds, they prevent neurons from transmitting messages to one another. In all cases of the disease, the hippocampus, a structure deeper within the brain between forty and fifty-two millimetres long, is affected first; it is essential for the retrieval of memories – especially recent ones – which is why, in the early stages of Alzheimer's, some sufferers can remember details from their past but cannot tell you what they ate for lunch.

To my surprise, I have taken some comfort from the clinical language of neurologists, who describe the brain as 'patterns of neural activations'.[50] Francis Crick, winner of the Nobel Prize for his collaborative work on DNA in 1962, described identity as follows: '"You," your joys and your sorrows, your memories and your ambitions, your sense of personal identity and free will, are in fact no more than the behaviour of a vast assembly of nerve cells and their associated molecules'.[51] While much of me revolts against such a factual description of the self, there is something I admire about neurological descriptions of the brain, which are unburdened by the ways that memory has long been associated in culture with identity. Or, as the neurologist David

Shenk puts it, 'We are the sum of our memories'.[52] Without memories, we live in a perpetual present, a condition which is paradoxically a state often championed by the advocates of 'wellbeing', but in its ultimate form it robs us of any sense of our past or awareness of our futures.

Every era, it seems, holds memory as central to a sense of being. For the philosopher John Locke, writing in the late seventeenth century, memory is inextricable from the sense of self. In contrast to the French mathematician and philosopher René Descartes, who famously stated in 1627 that 'I think, therefore I am', Locke effectively proposed 'I remember, therefore I am'. In 'An Essay Concerning Human Understanding' (1689), Locke argues that remembering what we did in the past is essential to our current sense of self. In other words, our identity stretches only as far as our memories reach back to the past. And before Gutenberg invented the printing press in the fifteenth century, memory was central to the political, social and cultural tenets of life. 'Worse than any loss in the body', wrote the Roman poet Juvenal in the first century AD, 'is the failing mind which ... cannot recognize the face of the old friend who dined with him last night, nor those of the children whom he has begotten and brought up'.[53]

The powerful connections between memory and selfhood notwithstanding, recent research on neurology deals a wild card that upends such clear-cut explanations. When we refer to memory, neurologists will point out that the term is a shorthand for a complex system made up of episodic memory, semantic memory, sensory memory, short-term and working memory, and prospective memory. And while we might believe that we have a vast storehouse of memories, the neuroscientist Rodrigo Quian Quiroga explains that, in fact, 'We remember almost nothing. The idea that we remember a great deal of the subtleties and details of our experiences ... is nothing more than an illusion, a construct of the brain.' What's more, 'the mere act of bringing up a memory to our consciousness inevitably changes it'.[54] And while memory has long been seen as an essential component of identity, as the philosopher William James argued in the late nineteenth century, 'In the practical use of our intellect forgetting is as important a function as recollecting'.[55] In Jorge Luis Borges's short story 'Funes the Memorious', the titular character suffers a bad head injury after falling off his horse. When he comes round, he realises that he cannot forget anything, a gift that soon becomes a curse. Forgetting, in other words, is an essential process, 'an active metabolic process, a flushing out of data in the pursuit of knowledge and meaning', a process that is increasingly necessary as we are overloaded with information.[56] As Baldwin puts it in *Giovanni's Room*, a slender novel in which the words 'remember' or 'remembered' occur more than fifty times, 'it takes strength to remember, it takes another kind of strength to forget', a process that has gained relevance with the relentless access to information in the digital age.[57] 'Perhaps dementia is the only response to a world in which all information is retained', Will Self posits. 'The individual has to obliterate this overload of data. Alzheimer's becomes the abiding condition of the human subject in a situation of total access to information.'[58]

~~~~~

Walking in the Dark is an attempt to navigate my own world in relation to my father's increasingly narrow sphere. In the thirty years that I have been reading Baldwin, his work has held a renewed relevance for me as I think about the world in relation to my father, and the perhaps unknowable world that his has become. One of Baldwin's late essays is titled 'Here Be Dragons', a phrase used by medieval cartographers to indicate unknown and dangerous territories, while another is called 'A Letter from a Region in My Mind'. As I have been thinking about my father's unchartered region in his mind, Baldwin's writing about memory, place, identity and illness has helped me to think through what it means to be untethered from the past, to be cut adrift from the memories that form us.

Although my two literary influences were born twenty years apart, and although they shared characteristics – heavy drinking, smoking, passionate arguing and a love of literature – this is not a book in which I compare the two men. Both have become, in different ways, spectral presences in my life. My father, who teemed with charisma, whose passion for literature, when fuelled with alcohol, could spill over into violence – though never physical – has become an incorporeal presence. Where once he bounded across a room, he has now forgotten how to walk and is uncertain of his surroundings, which confound him. Curtains are baffling and are not to be trusted. He peers behind them as though fearing the worst. A sudden change in temperature can cause alarm. Socks are to be discarded and washing is an ordeal that he must endure.

I've been stalking James Baldwin for thirty years, chasing traces of his life and work in archives, books and the various places where he lived, long after he died. There's something about the man and his craft – more than just charisma – that continues to draw me in. And while I admire the discipline of writers who plot their novels each morning, I'm drawn to Baldwin's rambunctious lifestyle, which frequently entailed drinking and debating throughout the night, followed by long bursts of whisky-fuelled writing. Despite his chaotic lifestyle, which saw him shuttling back and forth across the Atlantic, Baldwin's writing, at times lyrical and jagged, encourages us to think more deeply about race, politics, love, identity categories, memory and religion, often in unexpected and troubling ways.

Baldwin's life, like his writing, was complex and paradoxical. He was the most famous African American author of his generation, but he insisted on being described as an American writer. Baldwin was one of the most visible gay writers of his time, but he repeatedly denied the need for sexual categories. He was a child preacher who became a fierce critic of the church – and yet his work is shot through with kinetic spiritual energy. He was also a leading Civil Rights activist whose sexuality troubled Martin Luther King Jr., and whose polemics on race and love bemused and infuriated his peers. Baldwin was the most eloquent voice of his generation, a lone figure brimming with grace, rage and beauty, a stranger in the promised land of his birth, which he left in his early twenties.

My obsession with Baldwin has taken me far beyond the pages that he wrote. I've rummaged through his archive, where I've read drafts of his work, as well as his intimate, unpublished correspondence. And I've undertaken pilgrimages to his homes and haunts in New York City, France and Switzerland. In 2002, I visited the Cathedral of Saint John the Divine in New York City, where his funeral was held in 1987. Hushed by the cathedral's grandeur, I struck up a whispered conversation with the warden, who had yet to hear of Baldwin. I was reminded of the titles of his essays *No Name in the Street* and 'Nobody Knows My Name'.

Later that day, I wandered down to Greenwich Village where I installed myself in El Faro, one of Baldwin's favourite taverns. I sat in the far corner of the dimly lit bar, where

Baldwin held court in the 1960s, and I drank his favoured tipple – Johnnie Walker Black Label. On my fortieth birthday, I broke into his abandoned house in St-Paul de Vence, near Nice, searching in vain for a sign of this enigmatic writer, and several years ago I persuaded my wife to take a trip to Loèche-les-Bains, a small Swiss village surrounded by ice-capped mountains where Baldwin completed his first novel, hoping that it would lead to some kind of literary epiphany.

My fascination with Baldwin started before his current renaissance. By the time of his death, his reputation had dwindled. He was portrayed as an embittered writer of the Civil Rights Movement era whose work had suffered as he juggled the competing expectations of being a spokesman *and* a writer. Critics who were unsettled by his sexuality dismissed his 'sashaying' rather than penetrative prose. And then something remarkable happened to Baldwin's legacy. As the Black Lives Matter movement gathered momentum around 2014, Baldwin was resurrected; his maxims on police brutality and racism, a theme he revisited throughout his oeuvre, but which were given prominence during the Civil Rights Movement of the 1950s and 1960s, became despairingly relevant again. Along with those of his friends Martin Luther King Jr. and Malcom X, Baldwin's writing has flooded the X (Twitter) feeds of the Black Lives Matter movement. Between the 1940s and the 1980s, Baldwin's writing was frequently radical about race, sexuality and religion – in part because his views were edgy and unexpected. As Baldwin would have recognised, however, there is nothing radical – or enlightened – about reading or critiquing books in accordance with received ideas about sexuality, gender and race.

For the Twitterati, Baldwin is the voice of anger, a politicised writer whose eloquent range can be repurposed during America's new wave of racial violence. But this is only part of the story. His writing frequently resists categorisation and reduction, encouraging readers to think more deeply about the world around them. Baldwin, as I explore, was a writer who seemed to be in perpetual motion, whether travelling or quickstepping across the genres of fiction, non-fiction, plays and poetry. *Walking in the Dark* is my attempt to capture his restless brilliance, which continued to evolve. But I make no claims to cover all of Baldwin's work or themes; rather, the book is a way into thinking about that writer's work in relation to my father and thinking about my father in relation to Baldwin. At times, reading Baldwin helps me to make sense of my father's illness, just as my father's experience sometimes leads me to think more keenly about Baldwin, particularly around the themes that I address in this book – fathers, memory, home, illness and mistakes.

Baldwin is frequently described as a prophet, whose aphorisms have flooded social media, and are emblazoned on T-shirts, cushions and even prayer candles. But I am more interested in Baldwin's journey as a writer, which includes his errors and contradictions, as well as his unparalleled eloquence and insight. And while I dredge up and arrange memories of my father, it is tempting to curate a version of him that airbrushes out his faults, just as there is a tendency to discard digital photographs that show children crying or faces out of focus. Where possible, I have resisted any impulse to sanitise either man, as their complexity and con-tradictions are a vital part of their being.

I have a very early memory of sitting on my father's shoulders as we went in search of castles in mid-Wales. When I was a little older, I spent many summers walking and camping with him, sometimes just the two of us in the Brecon Beacons, where we wandered for hours until reaching local pubs. My father would make friends with everyone around

him, buying drinks for his new companions and telling me
I could eat whatever I wanted. While walking, my father
pointed out to me, was the best time to talk about difficult
and meaningful things, because it wasn't necessary to look
into someone's eyes or to be pinned down in a conversation.
The ebb and flow of walking eased the back and forth of
chatter and silence, and, in such moments, I felt at peace and
in tune with my father, and he with me.

In *Wanderlust*, Rebecca Solnit observes how, while walking,
'the body and the mind can work together, so that thinking
becomes almost a physical, rhythmic act', and how 'even
past and present are brought together when you walk as the
ancients did or relive some event in history or your own
life by retracing its route'.[59] For Henry David Thoreau, who
needed to walk at least four hours a day to preserve his health
and spirits, 'there is a subtle magnetism in Nature, which, if
we unconsciously yield to it, will direct us aright'.[60] Thinking
has long been associated with walking, from Aristotle and the
Peripatetic School to Jean-Jacques Rousseau, who explained,
'I can only meditate when I am walking. When I stop, I
cease to think, my mind only works with my legs.'[61] In *The
Dharma Bums* (1958), Jack Kerouac's third novel, walking is
a way of connecting to nature, but it is also a rejection of
rampant 1950s consumerism. As the narrator observes, the
free-spirited Japhy Ryder – a character based on the poet and
environmentalist Gary Snyder – 'doesn't need any money, all
he needs is his rucksack with those little plastic bags of dried
food and a good pair of shoes and off he goes and enjoys the
privileges of a millionaire in surroundings like this'.[62] During
the 1950s and early 1960s, as the Civil Rights Movement
ignited, Frank O'Hara's delicious *Lunch Poems* captured the
joy of walking through Manhattan and savouring the sights
and smells of the city. In 'A Supermarket in California', Allen

Ginsberg imagines strolling through solitary streets with Walt Whitman, who in turn records the joy of 'walk[ing], solitary, unattended'.[63] As Baldwin points out, however, 'Every black man walking in this country pays a tremendous price for walking', adding 'that marvelously mocking, salty authority with which black men walked was dictated by the tacit and shared realization of the price each had paid to be able to walk at all'.[64]

Recently, my father has stopped walking. He spends most of his time sitting in a high-back wooden chair. He has barely spoken for months, with the exception of telling someone to fuck off, and then telling my youngest sister that he loves her; for extended periods of time he says barely anything, then utters 'Heavens above'. Most people think of Alzheimer's as a disease that attacks the brain, but it also affects the body. Gait changes are often markers of cognitive decline. The last time I visited my father he had wandered off around the home. It took twenty minutes to find him. He is now at the still point of a turning world, his last steps taken. With little imprinted on his brain, it is up to those he leaves behind to remember him, and to remember for him.

In *No Name in the Street* Baldwin describes the scene of King's funeral. At one point, he finds himself walking with his old friends, the actor Marlon Brando and the singer Sammy Davis Jr. 'I had not been aware of the people when I had been pressing past them to get to the church', Baldwin recalls.

> But, now, as we came out, and I looked up the road, I saw them. They were all along the road, on either side, they were on all the roofs, on either side. Every inch of ground, as far as the eye could see, was black with black people, and they stood in silence. It was the silence that undid me. I started to cry, and I stumbled, and Sammy grabbed my arm. We started to walk.[65]

In *No Name in the Street*, Baldwin and his peers are pictured marching during the struggle for civil rights during the 1950s and 1960s. But marching is only one facet of movement in Baldwin's life and work. Walking, in Baldwin's writing, is variously solitary, dangerous, communal, metaphorical, but frequently hopeful. Or, as Ma Rainey sang it:

> I walked and I walked
> Till I wore out my shoes.
> I can't walk so far, but
> Yonder come the blues.[66]

Chapter 1

Fathers and illness

All that we are not stares back at what we are.

W. H. Auden, *The Sea and the Mirror: A Commentary
on Shakespeare's* The Tempest (1944)

Remember thee!
Ay, thou poor ghost, whiles memory holds a seat
In this distracted globe.

William Shakespeare, *Hamlet*

There's an essay by Baldwin that I find very hard to read in light of my father's illness. 'Notes of a Native Son', the title essay of Baldwin's first collection, from 1955, begins with an account of his father's death. On 29 July 1943, a few months before the birth of my own father, David Baldwin died, hours before his final child, Paula Maria, was born. Baldwin, the eldest child, turned nineteen on 2 August that year, which was also the day of his father's funeral, a day that was marked by a riot that broke out in Harlem. 'On the morning of the 3rd of August', Baldwin recalled, 'we drove my father to the graveyard through a wilderness of smashed plate glass'.[1]

The cause of the riot sounds distressingly fresh: after a white police officer, James Collins, shot and wounded Robert Bandy, an African American soldier, 3,000 Harlem residents protested outside the local police station. Six people died and some 600 were arrested in one of several riots that year. With echoes of the 'Red Summer' of 1919, when white-on-Black violence tore through American cities in the wake of the First World War, Black residents in Detroit, Beaumont, Texas, Mobile, Alabama and Los Angeles took to the streets. The anger stemmed from a confluence of actions that affected Black Americans during the war. As Baldwin knew only too well, workers, including many women, were placed in competition with each other in the war industries, and Black soldiers from the North deeply resented undertaking military training in the South. And in a ludicrous and cruel twist, Black soldiers could die for their country but were denied the same civil rights as their white compatriots.

Baldwin had a writer's knack of making events seem narratively right. 'It seemed to me', he recalled in 'Notes of a Native Son', 'that God himself had devised, to mark my father's end, the most sustained and brutally dissonant of codas', punishment the former child preacher believed, 'as a corrective for the pride of his eldest son'.[2] But Baldwin's account of the events surrounding his father's funeral does not quite add up: he recalls how the riot began shortly after his father's funeral, but it had in fact erupted the day before. The elision of dates notwithstanding, there is something striking about Baldwin's connection of his father, a man whom he described as a disciplinarian preacher, with the chaos that ensued shortly after his death, as well as a confluence of forces that resulted in death and life in the Baldwin family. It is not the account of David Baldwin's death that unsettles me, but his son's description of him during the last months of his life. In 'Notes of a Native Son', Baldwin describes how his father stopped eating, believing that his family were trying to poison him. 'When he was committed', Baldwin writes – although he does not tell us where – 'it was discovered that he had tuberculosis and, as it turned out, the disease of his mind allowed the disease of his body to destroy him'.[3]

Baldwin's description of his father's 'disease of his mind' is painfully reminiscent of my own father's brain, and, in particular, the changes to his hippocampus. Until my father's illness, I never thought much about the composition of the brain, or about the 'German disease', as my father called his condition in the early days. The clinical language that surrounds my father's illness – amyloid plaques and neurofibrillary tangles – sits at odds with my father, a man who scorned moderation and restraint, his infectious vitality akin to the Hippocampus of mythology, the fish-tailed horse of the sea.

It is Baldwin's account of his father becoming 'locked up in his terrors' that disturbs me as I think about my own father's deterioration.[4] Growing up, my sisters and I would joke about our father's inability to recall names, which proved challenging as a schoolmaster. His greeting of 'Hello, great man' or 'Hello, great woman' meant, we all knew, that he could not summon up a name. He got by, as he often did, with his extraordinary charisma. Around five years ago, he began forgetting more than just names. When my mother eventually cajoled him into speaking to a doctor, he was indignant about the dementia test, which he denounced as facile. He could not remember the name of the prime minister, he explained, because he couldn't stand 'that bloody woman', who, we reminded him, was called Theresa May.

My father's forgetfulness came on slowly at first. For years he had been a confident and safe driver. In the 1980s, my three sisters and I would be squashed together in the back of the rusty family car, while my father, with the panache of Lewis Hamilton, would overtake new BMWs on the motorway as he sang 'The green Saab don't take no prisoners'. It wasn't until I was in my twenties that I understood that most cars are designed for only three people in the back. For the most part, I sat crammed between my sisters with my parka zipped up like a sleeping bag as I tried to listen to The Cure while my father's voice boomed along the motorway.

Not being allowed to drive hit my father hard. He recalled confiscating the keys a decade earlier from his own father, who, after four strong gin and tonics, drove into the wall by his flat, damaging his knees and crushing the front of his small, fast car. For my grandfather, a decorated wing commander and survivor of numerous aerial skirmishes, the crumpled bonnet was merely 'a prang' and he, too, was reluctant to leave the cockpit.

My father complained bitterly about, and to, the DVLA and was determined to prove that he could drive again. His opportunity came quickly after my mother smashed her glenohumeral joint so badly that she required major surgery, a delicate operation to repair the shoulder's socket and ball. As he drove me to visit my mother in hospital shortly before his licence was rescinded, it was clear that his sense of perception had waned. He shouted at drivers who he perceived were cutting him up, and he cursed at the sound of car horns when he forgot to signal. It was a white-knuckle ride, as he once described his father's driving late in life – a journey and drama which played out the terrifying loss of control that my father was experiencing, his frustration at other drivers a last-gasp attempt to deflect the impending tragedy of his inevitable deterioration.

Keys, like jigsaw pieces, became a dominant motif during my father's decline. For a while he searched for the car keys that my mother had hidden. And then he became obsessed with his set of house keys, his bank card and his cigarillos. During his last year at home he would get up, check the location of the key, try it in the door, put it back, sit down and repeat. My mother would try to distract him from his task, but agitation and anger overpowered any attempt to divert my father. He became compulsive, fretful and frustrated, locked in his house, and locked up in his anxiety.

~~~~~

Baldwin describes how his father's illness led to him 'hating and fearing every living soul including his children who had betrayed him, too, by reaching towards the world which had despised him'.[5] As my father's illness took over his brain, he would tell my mother that he was going to kill himself. Slamming the door shut, he wandered out of their flat and into the heart of the market town where they lived. Sometimes he would return, usually with cigarettes, within ten minutes, but there was a period when he took to sitting with the local drinkers and homeless men and women. He wanted to sleep on the streets, he explained to my mother, and he wanted to help these people who had nothing, something which had always concerned both my parents. 'You see that man', he would say when I was young, pointing carefully to a figure we would often see walking the banks of the River Severn. 'He's a gentleman of the road; the richest man in Shropshire. Everything belongs to him.'

~~~~~

James Baldwin was in fact born James Jones. His mother, Berdis, was born in either 1902 or on Christmas Day the following year, on Deal Island off the coast of Maryland, also known as Devil's Island – a tiny inhospitable isle of around three square miles that is susceptible to flooding. Little is known about Berdis, who first appears on a census in 1940, where her birthplace is listed as Maryland, along with her age (thirty-eight). Softly spoken and reputed to have a brilliant mind and love of poetry, she was so petite that the writer Maya Angelou recalled she would have to stoop down just to kiss her on her forehead. At some point Berdis moved north in search of work, first to Philadelphia and then to New York City, where she gave birth in 1924, out of wedlock, to her first son, whom she called Jimmy.[6]

Baldwin was born as the New Negro Movement – or Harlem Renaissance as it was also known – was gathering momentum, an unprecedented flowering of Black American artistic and cultural production that lasted until the mid- to late 1930s. It was a period, as the writer Langston Hughes recalled, in which the 'Negro was in vogue', during which time Black American writers, artists and musicians, among them Zora Neale Hurston, Alain Locke, Jacob Lawrence and Louis Armstrong, displayed a new vision for African American culture and identity that would pave the way for the Civil Rights Movement.

Baldwin's arrival during the Harlem Renaissance notwithstanding, he rarely alluded to the cultural achievements of his forebears. Baldwin would often mention that he was moments away from being born in the South, a place that Berdis and so many of her generation fled. In the early twentieth century, after cotton crops were decimated by the boll weevil, an innocuous-looking insect with a long snout that devours cotton, and after biblical floods – as depicted in the 'Back-Water Blues', sung by Bessie Smith, one of Baldwin's favourite singers – African Americans looked for work in the northern cities of Detroit, Philadelphia, Chicago and New York. Pockets of northern cities, including Harlem, were populated, as Baldwin would have experienced, by people who had, like Berdis, been born in the South. The North was something of a promised land, where work could be found and where the threat of racial terror, including lynchings, was less pronounced. Berdis was part of the First Great Migration, when around 1.5 million African Americans refused to stay in the South, a land a whisper away from slavery where they endured Jim Crow segregation and relentless poverty.

Baldwin wrote about the American South in one of his earliest essays, 'Journey to Atlanta' (1948), which recounts a trip his brother David took as part of a gospel quartet in the mid-1940s, which, expanded and retold, was recast in his last novel, *Just Above My Head* (1979), in which one member of the singing troupe is murdered in the South, described elsewhere by Baldwin as the 'blood-stained land'.[7] In addition to essays such as 'Nobody Knows My Name: A Letter from the South' (1959), Dixie rears up in menacing ways in several of his other works, including his first novel, *Go Tell It on the Mountain* (1953), in which an unnamed Black soldier, a veteran of the Great War, is found beaten and castrated in the Deep South. 'The South had always frightened me', Baldwin states in his essay 'A Fly in Buttermilk' (1958), and he writes elsewhere that 'I felt as though I had wandered into hell' on his first trip there.[8]

Little is known about Baldwin's biological father. Of his first few years of family life, he recalled that 'I was the only child in the house – or houses – for a while, a halcyon period which memory has quite repudiated'.[9] When Baldwin was two or three years old, his mother met and married David Baldwin, a labourer and preacher from Louisiana who was one generation away from slavery. Baldwin recalls tugging at his mother's skirts to get her attention, because 'I was so terrified of the man we called my father, who did not arrive on my scene, really, until I was more than two years old'.[10] As Baldwin remembers, his stepfather moved in, along with his mother, Barbara, who had been born into slavery, and who was 'so old that she never moved from her bed'.[11]

Baldwin's recollections of his new father are couched in a language of hate, resentment and fear. David's first appearance in Baldwin's non-fiction takes place in 'Autobiographical Notes', the opening essay of *Notes of a Native Son*. His mother, Baldwin recalls, was 'delighted' with his early literary experiments, including plays and songs; his father 'wasn't', Baldwin explains, for 'he wanted me to be a preacher'.[12] Baldwin's brief description of his parents' responses to his early creative experiments sets the tone for his subsequent writing. Berdis, who 'was given to the exasperating and mysterious habit of having babies', is rarely mentioned.[13] She is there in fleeting memories of his impoverished childhood, where she 'fried corned beef, she boiled it, she baked it, she put potatoes in it, she put rice in it, she disguised it in corn bread, she boiled it in soup (!), she wrapped it in cloth...'.[14] Years later, when Baldwin was imprisoned for the theft of a bedsheet in Paris, he experienced a recurring nightmare involving his mother's fried chicken, in which 'At the moment I was about to eat it came the rapping at the door'.[15]

Mostly, however, Berdis is present in Baldwin's writing as a buffer between the aspiring writer and his strict and loveless stepfather. His mother 'paid an immense price for standing between us and our father', Baldwin recalls, adding that David knew how to make Berdis suffer.[16] And while his mother, who outlived her son, held the growing family together, it was David, an embittered evangelical, who looms in Baldwin's earliest writings. As one of Baldwin's biographers puts it: 'To the people of his house the father's prophecy took the form of an arbitrary and puritanical discipline and a depressing air of bitter frustration which did nothing to alleviate the pain of poverty and oppression'.[17] Beatings accompanied this 'bitter frustration' and his stepfather repeatedly told Baldwin that he was ugly.

By the time he had reached his thirties, Baldwin explained that he understood his father, who 'was very religious, very rigid', much better.[18] 'He wanted Negroes to do, in effect, what he imagined White people did', Baldwin recalls, 'that is to have – to own the houses, to own U.S. Steel'. But this frustration, Baldwin states, 'in effect, killed him. Because there was something in him which could not bend'.[19] Looking back over his childhood, Baldwin concludes that 'My father frightened me so badly, I had to fight him so hard, that nobody has ever frightened me since'.[20]

But if Baldwin found peace with his stepfather after his death, then his early writing was an exorcism of sorts, a way of seizing back control from the man who tyrannised his childhood. *Go Tell It on the Mountain* took him a decade to write. He lugged the tattered manuscript around during his early years working in New York and New Jersey, and then over to Paris when he flew to France in 1948, completing his debut work of fiction in the small village of Loèche-les-Bains, also known as Leukerbad, which is nestled high in the mountains in the canton of Valais in Switzerland. And while *Go Tell It on the Mountain* – the title borrowed from a well-known African American gospel – travelled across the Atlantic, surviving cheap Left Bank hotels in Paris and the journey to Switzerland, its subject was very close to home for the aspiring writer. The story, which draws heavily on Baldwin's childhood, takes place on a single day, the fourteenth birthday of John Grimes, who, like Baldwin, was expected to become a preacher, like his stepfather. But while the narrative present of the story is March 1935, the story moves back in space and time to the South and to before Baldwin was born. It was a novel, he explained, that 'I had to write if I was ever going to write anything else. I had to deal with what hurt me most. I had to deal, above all, with my father. He was my model; I learned a lot from him.'[21]

Baldwin's explanation of how he had to write *Go Tell It on the Mountain* is couched in a language of torn emotions. He had to deal with David Baldwin's cruelty – but he acknowledges that his stepfather, the source of his unhappiness, was also his model. In several essays Baldwin recalls how his stepfather controlled his children's lives. Jazz and blues music were forbidden by the zealous Baldwin Snr, as they were linked in his mind to a deviation from the path of the Lord. The cinema was viewed with great suspicion and so were white people. David Baldwin warned James 'that my white friends in high school were not really my friends and that I would see, when I was older, how white people would do anything to keep a Negro down'.[22]

Baldwin ignored his father's injunction to avoid befriending white people. At DeWitt Clinton High School in the Bronx, where he was one of the few Black students in a predominantly Jewish cohort, Baldwin's classmates included Emile Capouya, who later became literary editor of the *Nation*, and Sol Stein, a writer and publisher, as well as the renowned photographer Richard Avedon, with whom Baldwin edited the school's magazine, *Magpie*. But while he shared artistic pursuits with his non-Black classmates, his experience was distinct. He read voraciously, including Harriet Beecher

Stowe's bestselling novel *Uncle Tom's Cabin* and Charles Dickens's *A Tale of Two Cities*, 'over and over again', explaining that 'in fact, I read just about everything I could get my hands on – except the Bible, probably because it was the only book I was encouraged to read'.[23] But in contrast to his white friends, even searching out books could be menacing: 'Why don't you niggers stay uptown where you belong?' a police officer mutters to the thirteen-year-old Baldwin on his way to the library.[24]

In 'Autobiographical Notes', Baldwin pegs the King James Bible as one of his influences: his childhood was pulled in the direction of the Word and words. Between the ages of fourteen and seventeen, Baldwin became, as he later put it, a 'holly roller' preacher in a Pentecostal church. For his father, Baldwin's passion for reading and writing was a distraction from the way of the Lord, a tension that culminated in a terse conversation between the two of them when Baldwin was seventeen years old:

> My father asked me abruptly, 'You'd rather write than preach, wouldn't you?'
>
> I was astonished at his question – because it was a real question. I answered, 'Yes'.
>
> That was all we said. It was awful to remember that that was all we had *ever* said.[25]

The simplicity with which the tensions between Baldwin and his stepfather are resolved belies the years of struggle to reach that point. 'When he was dead I realized that I had hardly ever spoken to him', Baldwin recalled. 'When he had been dead a long time I began to wish I had.'[26] But it is the final two sentences of the above exchange that hit me most, a recollection that Baldwin wrote in the wake of his father's death: 'that was all we had ever said'. My own father, a ghostly presence of a man who was always so present in every room he occupied, is alive, but his memories of me have died. We can sound out words to one another, but we no longer converse beyond stop–start phrases. Each encounter with my father carries for me the burden of recognition when I believe, just for a moment, that he knows who I am, before these fleeting moments wither in the stale air of the care home.

I catch myself talking about my father in the past tense. How he used to delight in reading poetry and chatting to strangers; how he used to love pubs. Sometimes my father is silent, and I hang on every utterance as though he is an oracle emerging from a vow of silence. I lean in closely and notice that his teeth are stained and I wonder who brushes them for him. Is he compliant, like my toddler on a good day, or does he protest and push his carer aside? When he was eight years old, he lost his front two teeth playing cricket when his bat top-edged the ball from an older bowler. My grandmother once told me that he was still smiling through the blood and broken teeth. Now I feed him crisps, one at a time, which he seems to enjoy. When I pause to reach for a plastic cup of water, he continues the motions of eating, delicately placing invisible morsels into his now silent mouth.

I stare into my father's eyes and hope I can see a flicker of something that has survived the cruel efficiency of Alzheimer's. He is staring through me, through the walls of the home, and into a space I hope never to go. I am reminded of William S. Burroughs' description of a junky whose 'face wasn't blank or expressionless. It simply wasn't there.'[27] But my wife sees sadness in his eyes and I think she's right. My own eyes fill but I try not to cry, fearing this might upset my father. At one point he murmurs the name of my maternal aunt, who took her own life several years ago. Many years before, my father told one of my sisters that she should run him over if he suffered from dementia. He speaks a few words in French, takes my hand in his atrophied fingers and kisses the back of it with the delicacy of a courtesan. As we walk with him through the corridors, where Doris and her friends are swaying to an ABBA song, we are hit by the stench of piss and death, but also small moments of joy among the residents, as well as terror. 'The next time ...' my father says, and I lean in, hungry to take home a nugget of my father's old self. But words never come, and the incomplete sentence is cast away in the corridors of the home as I ponder the banality of Alzheimer's. I hug his bony frame and walk out without looking back.

~~~~~

In Baldwin's early writing, his stepfather is a menacing figure who radiates hostility as his stepson yearns for love. In 'The Death of the Prophet' (1950), Baldwin's first published short story, which appeared in *Commentary*, the leading post-war journal of Jewish culture, David Baldwin appears as Gabriel Grimes, the same name that Baldwin used for his protagonist's stepfather in *Go Tell It on the Mountain*. Baldwin's short story was forged in the crucible of his difficult relationship with David Baldwin. The central character, Johnnie, has left home and returns to visit his ailing stepfather, whose body is wracked with tuberculosis, and whose mind is possessed by a paranoia brought on by his fervent religiosity. In a flashback, Johnnie recalls how, after he had cursed God, 'His father stripped him naked and beat him until he lay on the splintery floor, in feverish sobbing and in terror of death'.[28] As the son of a prophet, Johnnie, like James, is forbidden to go to the cinema or the theatre, or to smoke or drink alcohol. 'It was not thought wise to read more at school than was absolutely necessary', Baldwin adds, 'for schools also, it had been revealed, might function as the anteroom to hell'.[29]

As Johnnie visits his father at home, he describes the man he called his father as a 'skeleton', his wrist 'a polished bone', a description, together with the 'sick sweet-sour' smell of the room, that brings to mind my own father, whose broad shoulders and robust frame are atrophied, his once expressive face sunk inwards. He has become like T. S. Eliot's 'Hollow Men' – 'In this last of meeting places / We grope together / And avoid speech'.[30] As Johnnie bids his father farewell, as the sound of 'Daddy' leaves the air, 'the skeleton became perfectly still. Then it seemed that there was no sound being made anywhere on earth'. The description ends with a line that haunts me as I think about my own father: 'Now communication, forgiveness, deliverance, never, the hope was gone'.[31]

Father–son relationships, often drawn from Baldwin's past, appear in other early writings as he struggled to complete his first novel, which was known, in early versions, as 'Crying Holy' and 'In My Father's House'. In 'The Outing', first published in 1951, two years before his first novel, Baldwin introduces characters drawn from his childhood through Johnnie, Roy and Gabriel. 'Roy's Wound', an excerpt from *Go Tell It on the Mountain*, was published in *New World Writing* in 1952, along with contributions by Norman Mailer, Jean Genet and Dylan Thomas. The title alludes to Gabriel Grimes's favourite son, who is stabbed in a fight, but the story is really about his stepfather's bitterness at his inability to provide for his family. In 'The Rockpile', a story that first appeared in *Going to Meet the Man* (1965), his only collection of short stories, Baldwin resurrects the characters of John and Gabriel in a tale that weaves in similar themes to 'Roy's Wound'.

Baldwin's various iterations of the story that he had to write suggest that he was haunted by the memories of his stepfather, and that writing was a way of confronting those demons, with the aim, perhaps, of achieving a sense of peace, or catharsis. As he put it many years after his stepfather's death, 'I have written but too much and too little about this man, whom I did not understand till he was past understanding'.[32] But the fact that David Baldwin keeps appearing in the form of Gabriel Grimes – a name that evokes both the ethereal and also the worldly – suggests that writing alone was not enough to exorcise these childhood memories. And just as Freud claimed that untended mourning can transform into melancholia, versions of David Baldwin continue to appear, his spectral presence leaking from fading memories across memoir and fiction. In *No Name in the Street*, written nearly thirty years after his stepfather's death, Baldwin describes his first memory of the man, who is smiling as he dries the dishes. 'I am apparently in my mother's arms', Baldwin writes, 'for I am staring at my father over my mother's shoulder, we are near the door; and my father smiles'. And yet, as Baldwin concludes, 'This may be a memory, I think it is, but it may be a fantasy'.[33]

Or perhaps it is the case that my reading of Baldwin is shaped by the circumstances of my own father, whose presence – and absence – haunts me when I visit him and fills me with guilt when I do not. I am struck by how much writing about haunting and hauntology seems to describe the condition of those with Alzheimer's – and certainly the condition of my father. Take this quotation from an early study of haunting from the late 1990s:

I used the term *haunting* to describe those singular yet repetitive instances when home becomes unfamiliar, when your bearings on the world lose direction, when the over-and-done-with comes alive, when what's been in your blind spot comes into view. Haunting raises specters, and it alters the experience of being in time, the way we separate the past, the present, and the future.[34]

In my father's case, in the months before he moved out of the flat he shared with my mother, their home had become resoundingly unfamiliar. He negotiated their small surroundings with uncertainty, which was compounded by the fact that my parents had not lived there long, and because his own father had lived there for the last fifteen years of his life. My father was once a keen walker and traveller, but his bearings were now shot, his inner compass broken as he wandered down once familiar but now alien streets. And like Hamlet, the eponymous character in one of his favourite plays, who remarks that 'The time is out of joint' after being visited by his father's ghost, my father's own sense of time is unfettered by chronology, a phenomenon known as time-shifting in people with Alzheimer's, many of whom are locked in the past. Time out of joint. People who have died can be presumed living by someone with Alzheimer's, while they may not always recognise friends and family, because they cannot summon up an image imprinted of them from the past.

For the French philosopher Jacques Derrida, the present is haunted by metaphorical ghosts of the future.[35] Or as Mark Fisher put it, 'The future is always experienced as a haunting: as a virtuality that already impinges on the present, conditioning expectations and motivating cultural production'.[36] When I visit my father, I am unsure whether I am haunted by the past – his memories and our experiences together – or whether I am terrified by what I will become in the future.

The past for my father is time out of mind, while for my family it remains time out of joint as we grieve for a man still living. My daughters have not met their grandfather, whose photographs they will learn to recognise, while for my sons, who remember my father's red trousers and love of ice cream, he is fading in their memories even as he lives.

I wonder if the persistent presence of Gabriel Grimes in Baldwin's early work is, at least in part, a way of dealing with his biological father, a man for whom no memories exist, who could not be mourned. In *If Beale Street Could Talk* (1974), the protagonist, Fonny, a young African American, languishes in jail after being falsely accused of rape. As the novel ends, it is unclear whether he will ever see his unborn child, who is carried by his lover, Tish. Echoes of illegitimacy and displacement abound in the titles of Baldwin's works: 'Nobody Knows My Name', *No Name in the Street* and 'Stranger in the Village'.

If David Baldwin, often in the guise of Gabriel Grimes, is a revenant in his stepson's fiction, then his recurrence is perhaps related to what could not be said. Much of Baldwin's early writing is preoccupied with young men navigating their way in unforgiving Christian households. In *Go Tell It on the Mountain*, John Grimes is drawn to an older boy, Elijah, who is at ease in his appealing body, and whose presence causes John's heart to pound and his palms to sweat.

As John thinks of older boys, Baldwin tells us that 'he had watched in himself a transformation of which he would never dare to speak', a reference, it seems, to the love that dare not speak its name. 'He would not be like his father, or his father's fathers', Baldwin writes. 'He would have another life.'[37]

Early drafts of *Go Tell It on the Mountain*, which can be seen in the Schomburg Center for Research in Black Culture, a research library in Harlem located near to where Baldwin grew up, are more explicit about the dizzying mixture of desire, religion and adolescence. As he showed the early drafts of his novel during the 1940s to the white friends his stepfather had forbidden him to see, they were struck by what they read. For the poet Harold Norse, whose career become entwined with the Beat Generation – he later became a leading gay-liberation poet – 'Crying Holy', as the novel was then called, was not only 'beautifully written', but 'It was the first time I had seen the subject of homosexuality in a contemporary novel'.[38] And for Baldwin's school friend Emile Capouya, the tattered manuscript had a clear message: 'I want a man'.[39]

It is not surprising that Baldwin toned down the explicitly queer content of his first novel. Not only was he a fledgling novelist, but publishers were cautious about printing books that could be accused of valorising homosexuality. For the editors at Knopf, who published Baldwin's first novel, his next offering, *Giovanni's Room* (1956), a bold novel about love between two men, was too risky. As one of Baldwin's biographers explains, 'A black writer was one thing; a black homosexual writer was simply too much for the public to bear'.[40] Gore Vidal's post-war novel *The City and the Pillar* (1948) was a courageous exploration of love between two men, but it ends in tragedy, a trope favoured by editors and publishers, as the implicit message is that homosexuals are punished in the end.

In his early work, including his short story 'The Outing', a title which might have drawn on the then new use of the term 'coming out', Baldwin hints at his protagonists' queer desire without articulating it. Read the story closely, however, and it is there, whispered across the pages as Baldwin tells of a group from the Harlem Mount of Olives

Pentecostal Assembly who take a trip on the fourth of July up the Hudson River. Johnnie is upset after a contretemps with his overbearing father, a strict church deacon, and seeks comfort in the arms of his friend, David. 'Your old man was kind of rough', David says. Johnnie agrees and, shivering, buries his face in David's shoulder. David holds Johnnie tighter:

'Who do you love?' he whispered. 'Who's your boy?'
'You,' he muttered fiercely, 'I love you.'[41]

The short scene is a beautifully rendered moment of intimacy between two teenage boys on the cusp of adulthood. Significantly, these moments of tenderness and burgeoning desire in Baldwin's early fiction nearly always take place in stolen moments away from the watch and wrath of the protagonist's evangelical father. There is no record, as far as I can tell, of whether David Baldwin knew about his stepson's sexuality, but it is likely that the aspiring writer kept it hidden, rather than risk, as he puts it in his first novel, being cast asunder 'with his sinful body, to be bound in hell a thousand years'.[42] It is also striking how the names of Baldwin's young protagonists give more than a nod to their biblical counterparts. In 'The Outing', the names David and Johnnie, as well as David and Giovanni (Jonathan) in *Giovanni's Room*, carry echoes of the Books of Samuel from the Old Testament. In the King James version, 'the soul of Jonathan was knit with the soul of David, and Jonathan loved him as his own soul', an utterance that is reminiscent of the relationship between David and Johnnie in 'The Outing'. 'Very pleasant hast thou been unto me', David tells Jonathan. 'Thy love to me was wonderful, passing the love of women.'[43]

Readers and theologians have long debated the nature of David and Jonathan's relationship. For Baldwin, however, the description in the Old Testament of love between two men must have been a way of working through his attraction to men from within a fiercely religious household. And in another echo, the relationship between the two young men in the Books of Samuel is menaced by Jonathan's father, Saul, King of the Israelites. Saul, concerned that his son is colluding with David to overthrow him, denounces Jonathan: 'do not I know that thou hast chosen the son of Jesse to thine own confusion'.[44] This precipitates a virulent dispute that ends with the father hurling a javelin at his son.

Notwithstanding his reputation as a pioneering writer of queer fiction, Baldwin rarely wrote about homosexuality in his essays, a form in which he frequently wrote as an authority on what it meant to be Black in mid-century America. To add sexuality into the equation, as Baldwin put it, explaining why he could not deal with Black queer sexuality in *Giovanni's Room*, was 'quite beyond my powers'.[45] And when Baldwin does discuss homosexuality, it is as a crusader against crude categories and straight-jacketed identities. In the second issue of *Zero* (1949), he dismissed tired arguments about queer desire as 'unnatural' in an essay called 'Preservation of Innocence', concluding with a fierce repudiation of labels, lest we 'all smother to death, locked in those airless, labeled cells, which isolate us from each other and separate us from ourselves'.[46] In an echo of 'Everybody's Protest Novel', in which he warned of the dangers of categorisation, Baldwin ends 'Preservation' with a warning against labels, or identity categories as they are now sometimes called. It is only in his late essay 'Freaks and the American Ideal of Manhood', published in *Playboy* magazine in 1985, that he shared his own experiences of being queer in his late teens, during which time he 'was getting on very badly at home'. It was a time, Baldwin recalls, when 'I was thrown out of cafeterias and rooming houses because I was "bad" for the neighborhood' and a period in which 'On every street corner, I was called a faggot'.[47]

'Freaks' is one of Baldwin's most candid accounts of his troubled teenage years. In the essay, there is a clear demarcation between the danger lurking in the streets and a different kind of hazard waiting for him at home. Baldwin recalls how, on one occasion, his father gave him the last dime in the house to buy kerosene, but he slipped on the icy streets and dropped the coin. 'My father beat me with an iron cord from the kitchen to the back room and back again', Baldwin writes, 'until I lay, half-conscious, on my belly on the floor'.[48]

It was a period in which Baldwin was, in his own words, 'certainly unbelievably unhappy and pathologically shy'.[49]

In much of Baldwin's work, he suggests that it is people who save one another, not religion or God. Before he left New York for Paris, he formed close friendships with two notable persons. Baldwin recalls meeting Eugene Worth in 1943 or 1944, around the time he was twenty years old. 'We were never lovers', Baldwin explains, but 'for what it's worth, I think I wish we had been'.[50] It was Worth, a member of the Young People's Socialist League, who politicised Baldwin in the early to mid-1940s. For a brief period, Baldwin was a Trotskyist, a rare moment in the writer's life when he pledged allegiance to a particular political movement. As he recollects in an essay called 'The New Lost Generation' (1961), Baldwin and Worth were comrades who 'carried petitions about together, fought landlords together, worked as laborers together, been fired together, and starved together'.[51]

Worth, Baldwin recalls, was his closest friend: a light-skinned African American 'whose future, it had seemed to all of us, would unfailingly be glorious'.[52] But then, unexpectedly, in 1946 Worth killed himself by jumping off the George Washington Bridge, an enormous structure that straddles the Hudson River, connecting Upper Manhattan to Fort Lee, New Jersey. Not long after Worth died, the port authority unfurled the largest free-flying American flag in the world from this bridge, a spectacle that would no doubt have riled Baldwin, who 'bitterly blamed the American republic' for his friend's death. Worth, Baldwin concluded, 'would not have died in such a way and certainly not so soon, if he had not been black'.[53] In one of his short stories, an unnamed African American narrator, a musician, returns to New York after living in Europe. As he approaches Manhattan, Baldwin describes how he 'had seen the flag which was nominally mine used to dignify the vilest purposes'.[54]

Recalling that he and Worth had quarrelled about love and politics on their last encounter, Baldwin was convinced for many years that he had hastened his friend's death. But his friend had other troubles. He was in love with a white woman, also a socialist, whose family had threatened to put him in prison, presumably because he was Black. Worth's death clearly had a profound effect on Baldwin, who recalls that if he had remained in New York 'he would [have] come to a similar end' – and indeed, within a decade, the writer would make the first of several suicide attempts.[55] Worth's death, Baldwin understood, forced him to understand that 'hatred, and the desire for revenge would reach unmanageable proportions in me, and that my end, even if I should not physically die, would be infinitely more horrible than my friend's suicide'.[56] Baldwin resolved to leave America, but the themes of suicide reverberate through his writing. In *Go Tell It on the Mountain*, Richard, a charismatic and irreverent young Black man, dies by suicide after a humiliating racially motivated police arrest. And in *Another Country* (1962), Baldwin's first bestseller, Rufus Scott, a jazz drummer who is partly based on Worth, is broken by the relentless cruelty of mid-century American racism. Early in the novel, Scott jumps off the George Washington Bridge and his suicide torments his friends and family for the remainder of the book. As Baldwin put it, Scott was 'the black corpse floating in the national psyche', whose suicide is prefigured in Langston Hughes's poem 'Suicide's Note', in which 'The calm, / Cool face of the river / Asked me for a kiss'.[57]

Baldwin wrote little about Eugene Worth, but enough for him to haunt his early writing. Around fifteen years ago, I became obsessed with trying to find out more about Worth, who seemed to be the missing piece in Baldwin's early political activity, a tragic figure who deserved to be more than a footnote in accounts of his now famous friend. In one of his essays, Baldwin wrote that his friend's body was found in the Hudson River, but I could find nothing to corroborate this claim. I contacted the New York Public Library to get hold of his birth and death certificates and was told that, surprisingly, Worth is not listed on the Social Security Death Index, at least under that name. I contacted the general manager of George Washington Bridge, a Mr Durando, in case there were records of those who had jumped from the bridge. He confirmed that records of suicides do not stretch back as far as 1946, explaining that many were lost on 9/11. He suggested that I try New York City's Police Department Harbor Unit, but they were unable to help. I spent an afternoon at the Schomburg Center where I pored over microfilm copies of the *Amsterdam News*, one of the oldest African American newspapers, but to no avail.

I began to wonder whether Worth, like Rufus Scott in *Another Country*, was a drummer, and I got in touch with the American Federation of Musicians, but again he eluded me. I spent three days in the Tamiment Library and Robert F. Wagner Labor Archives at New York University trying to locate a trace of Baldwin and Worth as Trotskyists at that time. After several days in an icily cold air-conditioned archive, in which I had searched for clues – including pseudonyms that the two friends might have used – I gave up. I remember the feeling of disappointment as I left the archive and wandered across Washington Square Park on a bright, hot day in May, where Baldwin and Worth likely strolled. The next day, I heard back from the Commissioner's Office of New York City, where I was informed by an employee that:

> I did not find the name Eugene Worth in the records of deaths reported in 1946–47; nor did I find it listed in the records of the Office of Chief Medical Examiner. And I believe it almost certain that the OCME would have been involved if the body had been found in New York City (but given the Hudson River currents, he could have wound up in New Jersey).

And then, finally, I found a record of Worth on the 1930 Federal Census (New York City, Brooklyn Borough) as an eight-year-old, his existence thereafter a mystery, with the exception of Baldwin's scant recollections.

My search for Eugene Worth probably tells me more about my own obsessions than any information about him was likely to reveal. There's a part of me that revels in the role of literary sleuth in such endeavours. Research is reminiscent of the art of puzzles that Georges Perec describes, in which 'The only thing that counts is the ability to link this piece to other pieces...'. But there is also a part of me that feels as though I am an interloper who has no right to disinter what has been buried. Some things are not meant to make sense or be known, just like Perec's Bartlebooth dies attempting to fill the final piece of a puzzle that is shaped like an X but the piece he holds is a W. In my puzzle, the missing piece, a W, eluded me.

~~~~~

In 1940, sixteen-year-old James Baldwin was at a crossroads. He was failing classes at DeWitt Clinton High School in the Bronx and he was in a sexual relationship with a Harlem racketeer (as Baldwin describes him) much older than himself. That year he also discovered he was illegitimate, after overhearing a conversation between his mother and David Baldwin, the man he assumed was his biological father. And to complicate matters, he was still a Pentecostal preacher, a role that he found increasingly difficult to maintain. Emile Capouya suggested that he meet a painter whom he knew in Greenwich Village called Beauford Delaney.

Baldwin recalls being terrified as he climbed the stairs to Delaney's Greene Street apartment in Lower Manhattan. He was greeted by a 'short, round brown man' in his thirties who had 'the most extraordinary eyes I'd ever seen'.[58] Delaney, who grew up in Knoxville, Tennessee, had moved to New York via Boston during the Harlem Renaissance of the 1920s and 1930s, where his colourful Modernist paintings hovered between abstraction and realism. Five years later, the writer Henry Miller celebrated the painter in his essay 'The Amazing and Invariable Beauford Delaney', but at the time Delaney met Baldwin he was a struggling painter (though he had come close to breaking through as a recognised artist over the previous decade). For the teenaged Baldwin, the meeting was a crucial moment in his life. Except for his former teacher, the poet Countee Cullen, Delaney was the first Black artist he had encountered, and he was also gay and the son of a preacher; Baldwin would describe Delaney as his 'spiritual father' and 'principal witness'.

Baldwin's recollections of Delaney suggest the ways in which the painter enabled the teenager to develop as a writer at a time, as he recalled, when he 'was getting on so badly at home that I dreaded going home'.[59] Entering Delaney's apartment, Baldwin was struck by the colours, but also by the sound. As the artist played records, Baldwin recalled that he 'began to hear what I had never dared or been able to hear. Beauford never gave me any lectures. But, in his studio and because of his presence, I really began to *hear* Ella Fitzgerald, Ma Rainey, Louis Armstrong, Bessie Smith, Ethel Waters, Paul Robeson, Lena Horne, Fats Waller.'[60] In stark contrast to his stepfather, who had forbidden blues and jazz lest the music lead his children into the darkness, Delaney showed Baldwin how this music was imbued with a complex spirituality.

Delaney's journals from the early 1940s suggest his profound influence on his young protégé. Lines such as 'The human stimulus of love ... is the great mover to growing consciousness' were echoed by Baldwin, who wrote, in the introduction to one of Delaney's shows nearly fifteen years later, 'I do know that great art can only be created out of love, and that no greater lover has ever held a brush'.[61] Delaney took Baldwin to concerts and galleries, all the while teaching the aspiring writer how to see. Baldwin recalls how, on one occasion, Delaney noticed 'a brown leaf on black asphalt, oil moving like mercury in the black water of the gutter, grass pushing itself up through a crevice in the sidewalk'. But as Baldwin looked again, seeing through his mentor's eyes, he understood that it was 'humbling to be forced to realise that the light fell down from heaven, on everything, on everybody, and that the light was always changing'.[62]

~~~~~

Growing up, I was distinctly aware of my father's confidence in his own body. He would stride naked between the bathroom and the bedroom he shared with my mother, singing Louis Armstrong songs and making up limericks. On one occasion, during a dramatic summer storm, he leapt outside butt naked with a bottle of shampoo and revelled in the rain as the family dog, Polly, danced around him, my father's voice bellowing across the garden.

In the early stages of Alzheimer's, my father clung to his clothes, refusing to change them or have them washed. My mother would wait until he slept, and then would whip his favourite trousers into the washing machine so as not to antagonise his increasingly volatile and unsure mind. Not wishing to change clothes and not wanting to wash are common symptoms in those with Alzheimer's. In my father's case, at times it seemed he wanted to cling onto his independence, but he also became terrified of change, which is not surprising, given the dark vicissitudes of his brain. When he moved into care, his clothes were frequently scattered across the home. He would appear with one sock on, or with just one shoe, as though defying the need for order. As he lost weight, his ill-fitting clothes became purely functional, a sharp contrast to his singular sartorial style of red trousers, bright green tweed suits and flamboyant jackets.

After a few months in care, my father refused to wear clothes at all. He would peel away the layers as though returning to a purer, timeless state. He wandered around the home, urinating where he pleased, refusing to be clothed. For a while he would go missing, only to turn up, snoring on a neighbour's floor or huddled in a cupboard in which his naked body lay curled like a question mark.

In several of Baldwin's early stories, there is a recurring theme of nakedness. In *Go Tell It on the Mountain*, John Grimes witnesses his father's 'hideous nakedness', a moment that he equates with the account in the Book of Genesis in which Ham saw the nakedness of his father, Noah, a transgression which leads to the patriarch cursing his grandson, Canaan, whose descendants were destined to perpetual servitude. And at the moment at which John Grimes is battling his salvation, Baldwin writes how 'His father's eyes stripped him naked, hated what they saw'.[63]

Baldwin's accounts of nakedness in his fiction, which are associated with shame and terror, stand in contrast to *Dark Rapture*, Delaney's earliest known portrait of the writer, painted around 1941. More than a dozen portraits of Baldwin by Delaney survive but it is this picture that captures the enigma of the aspiring writer, a moment in which he turned his back on his stepfather's wishes that he remain a minister and the year that he left home. In the portrait, a naked Baldwin sits in a bucolic scene far removed from the bustling Harlem streets and from his father's oppressive gaze. In this portrait, it is striking how comfortable Baldwin must have been in the company of his mentor, who captures the young man's enigmatic qualities in abstract brushstrokes that are poised between the realms of darkness and light, vulnerability and confidence.

Delaney rarely painted nudes, and his portrait of Baldwin suggests how important each artist was to the other. Delaney helped his young friend organise David Baldwin's funeral, and, in the absence of his biological father, and then his stepfather, the painter became an influential father figure in New York and then later in Paris from the early 1950s. Baldwin's writings about Delaney suggest that he taught him much about life and art: that jazz and the blues were as sacred as the gospel music they had both listened to in their respective youths; that there is an important difference between looking and seeing. But it was Delaney's letters to Baldwin about the importance of love that seem to resonate most clearly in the writer's work. 'Love is everything and releases magic and the marvelous in the face of gravest tragedy ... the shelter ... in which the miracle and honesty and the power of visions and continuity are housed', Delaney wrote to Baldwin in one letter. 'Learning to love is learning to suffer deeply and with quietness', he wrote in another.[64]

Delaney's belief in the transformative power of love was tested through much of his adult life as he endured crippling bouts of depression and self-doubt as an artist. In the early 1950s, at the age of fifty-two, he moved to Paris to be closer to Baldwin, a city that offered some relief from the oppressive racism he had endured in New York. At times, Delaney's behaviour was eccentric. On one occasion he hid a painting under his bed because he refused to sell it to a buyer whom he did not like, even though he was barely able to afford the tools of his trade. And then, in an echo of my own father, who began to experience visions and delusions, Delaney's behaviour became increasingly erratic as he experienced prolonged bouts of paranoia, which included him hearing increasingly noisy voices around him.

By the early 1970s, as Alzheimer's disease found its way into Delaney's brain, the spiritual father was increasingly in need of support from his spiritual son. He was under doctor's orders to abstain from alcohol, an order he likely forgot or ignored, just like my own father, who gulped with gusto after he had replenished his guests' glasses. 'Everything in moderation is immoderate' he would tell me as he uncorked a third bottle of wine. In the last year before he left home for a new kind of home, my father forgot that he had given up smoking, something which gave him a shored-up pleasure, even as I worried about where he would discard his cigarette ends. Towards the end of his time at home he no longer realised that he was being plied with non-alcoholic beer and wine.

As he neared death, Delaney, as his biographer puts it, 'could not cope with the details of life'.[65] Lord knows how disorientating it must have been for Delaney as the voices and paranoia coiled around his diseased brain. And while Baldwin helped with his finances and hospital appointments, there must have been long periods when he was alone, confused and terrified. In my father's case, my mother's love and patience helped to anchor him, even as he became increasingly unmoored. He sought out the company of the displaced, just as Delaney's apartment in France became overrun by squatters. For Delaney, a native of Tennessee, I wonder how he fared as his memory failed him, and how much the French language added to his bewilderment.

Delany died in 1979, eight years before Baldwin, and the year in which his spiritual son published his final novel, *Just Above My Head*. Towards the end, Delaney's biographer observes that he 'simply stopped fighting' and took no interest in painting, just as my father has no interest in books, his lifelong passion.[66] I am not sure that Alzheimer's can be fought, however, or defeated. It is a meta-disease of sorts in which the brain suffocates the brain, slowly strangling itself until the body is ruptured from the mind. And unlike the peace that death can bring, this disease haunts those that it leaves behind, whose mourning begins before death arrives. There is an achingly beautiful photograph of Baldwin and Delaney taken a year before the painter's death. Both men are glancing to their left. Baldwin, looking like a rock star in sunglasses and hip top, is clasping Delaney's left hand, their fingers meshed, while the painter's left hand grips his hospital gown, as though holding on for support. Baldwin's gaze is commanding, even through his sunglasses, while Delaney's once keen eyes are unfocused, adrift. When his mentor died the following year, Baldwin did not attend the funeral, explaining that he was 'acting like a spoiled son somehow angry at his father for dying without his permission', which is reminiscent of the feelings I have towards my father's long, now silent death.[67] I find reasons not to visit him in the care home, which is an experience that fills me with fear and guilty revulsion. Letting go, when hands are interwoven, and when life imitates death, is not easy, just as echoes of my father remain just above my head.

Chapter 2

Writing home

Home is memory.

Toni Morrison, *The Source of Self-Regard: Selected Essays, Speeches, and Meditations* (2019)

Architectural Digest, 'The International Magazine of Fine Interior Design', has been gracing coffee tables for over 100 years. I have never met anyone who professes to be a regular reader of this slick periodical, but it's clearly imprinted in my imagination. I picture sharply dressed couples who sip Honduran natural-processed coffee as they peruse the pages and hold serious discussions about the beautifully photographed interiors. The August 1987 edition of *AD*, as I imagine some readers call it, is a must for anyone interested in Romantic Modernism. It features 'A New York apartment to refresh the senses', and there is a profile of Ethel Kennedy, the widow of Senator Robert F. Kennedy, with photographs of her patrician drawing room, which resembles a cross between a museum and a country club. It would be easy to miss the short piece written by James Baldwin, accompanied by seven sumptuous photographs of his home in the south of France, which is one of several featured articles.

The fact that Baldwin is not mentioned on the cover of *AD*, or even featured prominently in the magazine, tells us something about his reputation during the last few years of his life. Writing in the *New York Times* in the late 1990s, Michael Anderson even suggested that 'Baldwin's significance ended in 1964 with the artistic and commercial failure of his agitprop play, *Blues for Mister Charlie*', which anticipated a swathe of indictments about the writer's so-called failing craft over the next two decades.[1] (In sharp contrast to Mr Anderson's post-mortem, the writer Amiri Baraka claimed that Baldwin's play 'announced the Black Arts Movement'.[2]) The year before his supposed fall from stylistic grace, however, is often seen as the apex of Baldwin's career. On 17 May 1963, the writer was featured on the front cover of *Time*, a weekly news magazine that was founded around the same time as *AD*, with a circulation of over two and half million. In the foreground, a painting of an earnest-looking Baldwin wearing a tan-coloured shirt stares out. Behind the image of the writer, the white background is interrupted by black zig-zagged lines below a banner with the words 'Birmingham and Beyond: The Negro's Push for Equality', which cuts across the top-left corner.

The *Time* cover positions Baldwin as a serious writer who is a stalwart of the Civil Rights Movement, and yet the unnamed author of the article manages to undermine his subject with sly under-the-table kicks. Baldwin 'is not, by any stretch of the imagination, a Negro leader', the article explains, before launching into a description of the writer that tacitly acknowledges his sexuality in a way that undermines his suitability as a Civil Rights activist. 'He is a nervous, slight, almost fragile figure, filled with frets and fears', the anonymous journalist writes, as though Baldwin was the heroine of a nineteenth-century novel. 'He is effeminate in manner, drinks considerably, smokes cigarettes in chains, and he often loses his audience with overblown arguments.'[3]

Notwithstanding the barbed piece in *Time*, which joins a long list of articles that ooze discomfort with the writer's race and sexuality, Baldwin had certainly made it. A week later, he was invited to discuss race relations with Robert Kennedy, who would appear on the cover of *Time* the following month. The unofficial meeting took place at the senator's apartment at 24 Central Park South, Manhattan, a recently completed building designed by Philip Birnbaum, the architect later responsible for designing Trump Towers. After the publication of his third novel, the bestselling *Another Country*, the year before, and with two earlier collections of essays gaining traction, Baldwin was fast becoming a celebrity writer, underscored by the commercial and critical success of *The Fire Next Time*. Baldwin brought along a group of his friends and acquaintances to Kennedy's apartment, among them the singer Lena Horne, the entertainer Harry Belafonte, the playwright Lorraine Hansberry, and Jerome Smith, a young Freedom Rider who had been beaten to within an inch of his life on the frontline of Civil Rights battlefield. The meeting ended badly, when Kennedy suggested to Baldwin and his peers that the Irish had also suffered discrimination. Hansberry left the meeting in disgust and Baldwin was incandescent with rage at the US attorney general, a white millionaire and brother of the president, who claimed he had suffered persecution. Kennedy concluded that Baldwin was 'a nut' and he gave orders for the writer to be surveilled by the FBI, a move that led to the Bureau amassing a dossier of nearly 1,800 pages.

One hundred years after his birth, Baldwin seems to be everywhere, from academic monographs to aphorisms culled from his essays and shared on social media. He even makes a cameo role in Marvel Studios' film *Spider-Man: Homecoming* (2017), albeit in poster form on the wall of the classroom where Peter Parker is stuck in detention. Amid the cacophony of decontextualised quotations of Baldwin's work it is easy to forget that the writer did not fare well during the 1970s and 1980s. Had social media existed then, he would not have had many followers. His last novel, *Just Above My Head*, was published to lukewarm reviews in 1979, and he was increasingly seen as *passé*, a relic from the Civil Rights era who was pictured carousing with Nina Simone and Miles Davis in the south of France, rather than focusing on his craft or shaking his fist at the white Establishment. 'I am not in exile and I am not in paradise. It rains down here, too' Baldwin said with laconic understatement in interviews, aware that readers were beginning to doubt his credentials to speak about American politics from a villa in the hills above Nice.[4] Friends and biographers recall Baldwin talking about his 'comeback' during the 1980s, but it never occurred. Baldwin's insight and charisma never left him, but he found it harder to sustain the flinty, penetrating prose that had cut deep into the fabric of American society during the preceding decades. I met someone in 2010 who had heard Baldwin describe the writing process of one of his best essays, published in October 1953. Baldwin explained that he wrote 'Stranger in the Village' in a week and that he spent the rest of the summer editing it. Twenty years after that pitch-perfect essay, Baldwin had stopped taking interest in his craft. As the writer Caryl Phillips put it in a trenchant essay about his friend, 'if you refuse to edit your own book then you have either lost faith in the book, or you have lost sight of the importance of writing'.[5]

I've been trying to avoid writing a declension narrative in which Baldwin's brilliance, like my father's vitality, atrophies, but there are moments when it is difficult to avoid this trap. In dementia studies, 'dementism' refers to the bias against old age and impaired cognition, just as ageism sees change as a deterioration, rather than simply another stage of life. Search for synonyms of ageing and the thesaurus will throw out 'crumbling', 'fading', 'declining' and 'decaying'. Baldwin made a splash as a young dynamic writer in the 1950s, and there's a common perception that his writing had lost its way by the mid-1960s, during which time he was torn between his desk and the rostrum. In my reading of Baldwin's work between the 1940s and the 1980s, his fierce intelligence did not wane; there are some stunning set pieces in his later novels, but they are not supported by tight structure or clear plotting. In his late work, those distinctive Baldwin sentences – tightly coiled phrases buttressed with commas on the subject of love, religion and friendship – become fleeting, coordinates for readers to find a way back to the writer's early work. I find it hard not to compare the end of an early Baldwin essay from the late 1950s – 'The Discovery of What It Means to Be an American', which ends with the line 'Though we do not wholly believe it yet, the interior life is a real life, and the intangible dreams of people have a tangible effect on the world' – with his article on interior design thirty years later.[6]

But Baldwin, like my father, never lost his capacity to surprise. The article in *AD*, written by Baldwin, rather than a journalist, is full of insight about home and place, a now popular, even fashionable strand of non-fiction writing. Every story is set somewhere, but the current interest in place writing generated by authors such as Robert Macfarlane, Horatio Clare and Amy Liptrot is perhaps informed by a collective sense of uncertainty: about what place means in the landscapes of globalisation and neoliberalism, and anxiety about the very future of the place in which we dwell in an era of climate emergency. For Baldwin, as he explains in *AD*, home was often precarious, a transitory space. His dwellings included Manhattan apartments on the Lower East Side and Upper West Side after he left home. In Paris, he lived in numerous abodes, including the Left Bank Hotel Verneuil, which is now a quaint boutique guest house, and then an apartment in Clamart, south of the capital, where Beauford Delaney had moved in 1953. There was a dalliance with an apartment in Corsica; he rented a flat in Chelsea, London, during the late 1960s; and he spent an intermittent decade in Istanbul during the 1960s. In 1965 he bought an apartment for his family on the Upper West Side of New York City, where his mother, two sisters and their children lived, a permanent residence that served as the family 'headquarters' until his death.[7] But, as Baldwin explained, 'I never expected to "stay" in these places. I never expected to *stay* anywhere. I was a kind of transatlantic commuter, carrying my typewriter everywhere, from Alabama to Sierra Leone to Finland'.[8]

~~~~~

In one of the most poignant scenes captured in the documentary *James Baldwin: The Price of the Ticket* (1989), Baldwin's brother David delivers a moving epitaph on his brother's legacy. Born seven years after his brother James, and the youngest of four Baldwin brothers, David, who was variously an actor and bartender, remained close to his famous sibling and he was there when called upon to provide support. (At the infamous gathering with Robert Kennedy, David Baldwin shook his fist in the attorney general's face.) In the documentary, David speaks as though channelling his recently departed brother, employing a poetic language hewn from the scriptures on his brother's last thoughts:

> He said, 'I pray I have done my work so that when I have gone from here – and all turmoil, through the wreckage and rumble, and through whatever – when someone finds themselves digging through the ruins,' he said, 'I pray, that somewhere in that wreckage they'll find me; that somewhere in that wreckage that they can use something that I left behind. And if I've done that, then I've accomplished something in life.'[9]

James Baldwin's humble meditation on his legacy invites readers to become archaeologists sifting through his life and work, an act which carries echoes of Toni Morrison's notion of the writing process in her essay 'The Site of Memory'. Thinking through the ley lines that connect autobiography, history and fiction, Morrison employs what she calls 'literary archaeology' to imagine the interior life of enslaved people whose subjectivity has been erased from history.[10]

Baldwin's hope that readers will sift through the wreckage of his life was imbued with renewed relevance as I helped my mother sort through my father's papers and possessions in the wake of the ruins of his brain after he moved into a care home. My father had a near pathological aversion to paperwork, which became more pronounced when he retired from his job as a schoolmaster. My mother had to coax and then force him into signing the relevant paperwork for his pension, money that now pays for his care. After retirement, he gave numerous public lectures on a range of subjects – First World War poetry, Frederick Douglass, Maya Angelou, Jane Austen, Mark Twain and Nancy Mitford – but each talk only added to his anxiety when it came to filling out his annual tax return. The tax forms lay in disarray on his dark wooden desk – which I now use – hidden under coffee cups, wine glasses and ash trays.

As I helped my mother clear out my father's papers, I came across piles of his lecture notes, including a talk that he gave on John Betjeman, whom he had met while a schoolboy. In a brief encounter with the poet laureate sometime in the 1950s, my father informed him that he wrote good verse, rather than poetry, an anecdote he prefaced by referring to the arrogance of youth. Digging in the drawer by my parents' bed, which made me feel nervous about what I might find, I came across one of the first articles I had published on Baldwin twenty years ago. The margins of the article were crowded with my father's distinctive handwriting, a tightly wound elegant script that carried his precise use of language perfectly. One of my father's former colleagues wrote to me not long ago, reminiscing about his 'infinite energy' and humour, as well as his linguistic precision. 'I remember him picking me up once when I said I must do something, I forget what', Tom recalled. '"Must?" he said, and I have tried ever since not to use that word loosely.' My father did not write to me often and I wish I had kept his warm and amusing missives, especially now that he cannot hold a pen or read a page.

My father was not a sentimental man and he cared little for possessions. At some point during my childhood, on a whim he bought a sword stick in an antique shop. When a family friend told him that she liked it, he gave it away without hesitation, his actions unfettered by a desire to save money, or to keep possessions if they might bring happiness to someone else. He amassed a library of books on poetry, psychoanalysis, architecture and history, and he was quick to give away any title if he thought it would interest a visitor or student. And while he was a deeply social creature who needed company, which he often fuelled with wine, he left our home on a number of occasions to spend time alone, including retreats to Trappist monasteries. In later years, he would set off on his small canal boat, alone but for whisky and his dog – an only child, I always thought, who did not quite understand family.

When his mother died, she left behind a large folder with newspaper cuttings about her only son, which I collected into a book. There were articles about my father's football matches as left back for England School Boys, a team in which Ryan Giggs and Michael Owen later played, as well as pieces about him acting in plays as part of the Footlights, a longstanding student sketch-comedy troupe, at the University of Cambridge. When I presented him with the scrap book, he thanked me, but I don't recall him looking through the pages, or mentioning it again. I don't remember my father talking much about the past, or about his tense and fraught home life. His mother, the daughter of a druid from Suffolk, had gained a scholarship to Oxford at the age of fifteen. Her parents would not let her go because they could not afford the cost while they struggled to look after her seven siblings. She became a governess and then English tutor, her keen mind never quite recovering from what might have transpired at university. My paternal grandfather abandoned his studies as a veterinary surgeon in London to join the Royal Air Force. 'I had to, old boy', he told me once over his third gin and tonic, reminding me that his initials were R.A.F.

My mother told me about the long and difficult boozy lunches that my father had endured as a schoolboy during the holidays. His mother, an avid reader with a sharp mind, selected poems which were dissected over the course of the meal. The three of them sat on the same blood-red, velvet-clad dining-room chairs at a time when social formality extended to family interactions. With little interest in reading or discussing poetry, my grandfather drank a lot and said little. He was an avid smoker who grew a moustache, he explained to me, so that he could keep puffing while he shaved. The three of them must have had fun at times: each had a pilot's licence when my father was eighteen, but the dining room was a fraught territory. And while my grandfather seemed to me a kind and diminutive grey man who was passionate about growing peppers, rather than discussing poetry, he was not a stranger to wit. On one occasion he fell asleep at a high-profile RAF dinner, events at which drinks were plentiful. 'Wing Commander Field', boomed a voice that roused him from his Armagnac-induced slumber. 'What's your opinion on this matter?' 'I agree with the last person's views', muttered my grandfather, only to be told that he was the first respondent. 'In which case, I agree with the next person' he declared, before drifting back to sleep.

In the dining room, they would have eaten my grandmother's meticulously planned meals that were presented as works of formalist art. Grapes were always peeled and de-seeded, and the prawns were arranged symmetrically on floral china plates, each with a story of their respective provenance. During the 1980s, she refused to buy a washing machine, continuing to mangle their clothes because she would not buy anything from Japan, a reaction to the four years her brother spent in a Japanese POW camp. He did not speak about his ordeal except to explain that he survived by brewing a tea from white chrysanthemum flowers. My grandmother refused all offers of help around the house, her face flushed with the exertion of maintaining her own impossibly high standards, her cheeks a shade away from vermilion after her second gin martini. After three drinks, she became dangerous, and she began to resemble the pressure cooker that hissed in her tiny kitchen as she confused my father by oscillating between affection and accusation.

My grandmother was never cruel to me, but I was wary of her, nonetheless. She would kiss me on both cheeks when I arrived to stay, the start of a ritual which involved clasping my young head in her soft hands, pulling my head back slightly and gazing right through me. Even now, I if catch the bass notes of her perfume, I feel her presence. She had something close to psychic powers, a gift she inherited from her mother, who dabbled with a crystal ball – and she could always tell when I was lying. Unlike my father, I was spared her cruelty and was rewarded with affirmations. Two of my sisters did not fare so well. One year, as the result of a perceived slight – perhaps because our grandmother had not received a thank-you letter for a birthday present – my oldest sister received a Mars bar for Christmas while her siblings each received a book. On another occasion, my middle sister was reduced to tears, which gave me an insight into my father's vulnerable childhood. 'Leona is the oldest child, which makes her special. Douglas is the only boy, which makes him special. Annabel is the youngest child, which makes her special. So where does that leave you, Miranda?'

At the age of six and a half, my father was despatched to boarding school as Wing Commander Field was stationed abroad; the school fees were paid by the Royal Air Force. He must have lived in Italy during his first few years, as I remember my grandmother telling me that his first words were in Neapolitan, but these details, like so many others, are shadow facts that can no longer be corroborated. I know that he also spent early years in Luxor, Egypt, and that he first swam – or floated – in the Nile, but these details are untethered and perhaps irretrievable.

Shortly after my paternal grandfather died, my father started giving away his possessions, among them an old Browning camera, which he gave to one of my brothers-in-law, a keen photographer. As he tinkered with the camera, he noticed a roll of film tucked inside, which he managed to develop. There were over twenty pictures of my father, aged around four, in various poses with his parents, who must have been living in Naples. The pictures, though taken around 1948, remind me of staged Victorian family portraits. In one, my father plays the piano; in another he wears his father's Royal Air Force cap. He is pictured reading on a patterned sofa, lying on his stomach in a smart pair of shorts, his dark curly hair resisting the comb's recent assault, while his legs flop happily behind him. In three of the pictures, he is held by his adoring mustachioed father, who looks handsome and proud in his meticulous uniform. Fifty years later, as he looked at these photographs, which captured instants from his distant past, these fixed moments of fleeting happiness reminded my father of his father's attempts at affection.

〜〜〜

Baldwin is known as the most eloquent voice of the Civil Rights Movement and for his bravery as a writer who refused to remain in the closet when it was dangerous to be Black, hazardous to be homosexual and perilous to be both. Baldwin's work, much like his article for *AD*, is also saturated with insightful meditations on home and place, themes which echo within his writing. He was a self-styled 'trans-Atlantic commuter', having left the United States for Paris in 1948, remaining in France for most of his life.[11] He also spent an interrupted decade, spanning the 1960s, in Turkey, a country with which he felt a deep connection. 'During my stay in Istanbul', Baldwin explained, 'I learned a lot about dealing with people who are neither Western nor Eastern'. Living among people 'whom nobody cares about', Baldwin recalled, '[y]ou learn about the brutality and the power of the Western world'.[12] Although Baldwin died in St-Paul de Vence, near Nice, his home for the last seventeen years of his life, he dismissed claims that he was an expatriate writer, reminding readers that he had never relinquished his American passport. 'You never leave home. You take your home with you', Baldwin insisted. 'You better. Otherwise, you're homeless.'[13]

That the working titles for *Go Tell It on the Mountain* included 'Crying Holy' and 'In My Father's House' and that 'Notes of a Native Son' was originally published in *Harper's Magazine* with the title 'Me and My House' indicate the significance of home for Baldwin. 'But as for me and my house', Baldwin recalls his stepfather declaring, 'we will serve the Lord'.[14] In Baldwin's early work, the concept of home is frequently intertwined with the church, or house of prayer, as it was also known, which is not surprising given that Baldwin recollected leaving the church and home on the same day.

In his later work, Baldwin explores the connections between the familial home and the metaphorical house of America, in which African Americans live in cramped servants' quarters. 'This is your home', Baldwin tells his nephew in *The Fire Next Time* (1963). 'Do not be driven from it', Baldwin writes, drawing on the Gospel of John. The King James Bible contains the lines 'In my Father's house are many mansions' – here meaning rooms – 'I go to prepare a place for you'.[15] The first part of *Nobody Knows My Name: More Notes of a Native Son* (1961), Baldwin's second volume of essays, is called 'Sitting in the House'. Here and elsewhere in Baldwin's writing, references to houses and rooms connect the familial home to broader questions about American history. Towards the end of 'A Letter to My Nephew', first published in *The Progressive* magazine in December 1962 – and then retitled ('My Dungeon Shook: Letter to My Nephew on the One Hundredth Anniversary of the Emancipation') and used as a preface to the main essay ('Down at the Cross: Letter from a Region of My Mind') of *The Fire Next Time* – Baldwin quotes from the spiritual 'Tree of Life', also known as 'Hold On', where the cellar he recalls from his childhood home is transformed into a symbol of racial emancipation: *'The very time I thought I was lost, My dungeon shook and my chains fell off'*.[16] The title of one of Baldwin's late essays, 'Notes on the House of Bondage', draws on the Old Testament stories of Jews fleeing slavery in Egypt, tales which became linked in African American culture to their own slavery and freedom.

Raoul Peck's Oscar-nominated and BAFTA Award-winning documentary *I Am Not Your Negro* (2016) took inspiration from a manuscript that Baldwin had barely begun. Towards the end of his life, Baldwin was attempting to write a book about three Civil Rights leaders – Malcolm X, Martin Luther King Jr. and Medgar Evers – all of whom were murdered during the 1960s. As he explained in *No Name in the Street*, his writing had been interrupted by 'trials, assassinations, funerals and despair'.[17] The essay concludes with a list of places where the book was composed, giving the reader an insight into Baldwin's peripatetic lifestyle: 'New York, San Francisco, Hollywood, London, Istanbul, St-Paul de Vence, 1967–1971'. Perhaps some things are too painful to write about. The book that remained in note form, an account of his friends' assassinations, was titled *Remember This House*.

In *The Fire Next Time*, Baldwin famously asked, 'Do I really *want* to be integrated into a burning house?' – an image that became increasingly relevant following the publication of his book. There was mounting violence in Birmingham, Alabama, during the summer of 1964, while over 3,000 arrests were made during the Watts riots the following year. During the 'long, hot summer of 1967', as it became known, more than 150 riots erupted across US cities.[18] Baldwin's shifting senses of home and place are captured during a talk that he gave at the West Indian Students' Centre, London, in the late 1960s:

> That great Western house I come from is one house, and I am one of the children of that house. Simply, I am the most despised child of that house. And it is because the American people are unable to face the fact that I am flesh of their flesh, bone of their bone, created by them. My blood, my father's blood, is in that soil. They can't face that. And that is why the city of Detroit went up in flames. And that is why the city of Saigon is under martial law.[19]

Footage of the speech, shot by the Trinidadian film director Horace Ové, shows Baldwin in full command of the audience, made up of West Indian students and intellectuals. He is at the height of his rhetorical powers, his skills honed in the pulpit as a teenager and then perfected during countless interviews during the 1960s.

Baldwin begins his talk with a revealing anecdote. He recalls meeting a West Indian man in London, who asks him where he's from. When Baldwin explains that he is from Harlem in New York, the man keeps asking until it's clear he wants to know about the author's African heritage. 'I tried to explain', Baldwin tells the audience, 'that if I were originally from Dakar or from wherever I was from in Africa, I couldn't find out where it was, because my entry into America is a Bill of Sale'.[20]

While Baldwin's writing was not static, there are familiar themes that echo and reverberate throughout his body of work, which began in the 1940s and ended in the mid-1980s. His early work discusses the recent Second World War and his later work makes references to Michael Jackson and Boy George. During these four fast-changing decades, however, Baldwin remained steadfast in his view that he was American, and had little connection to his African forebears. In the poem 'Heritage', published a year after Baldwin's birth, his old French teacher, Countee Cullen, had asked the question 'What is Africa to me?', which haunts much of his star pupil's writing about the continent.

Baldwin's move to Paris intensified his writing about home. Not yet in his mid-twenties, the aspiring writer no doubt missed his siblings, his adoring mother and her home-cooked food. Arriving in the French capital, he followed a well-trodden path of Americans settling in or passing through the City of Light, among them Ernest Hemingway, F. Scott Fitzgerald, Gertrude Stein and Djuna Barnes. African American writers and artists, including the author Richard Wright, the cartoonist Ollie Harrington, and the writer Chester Himes, found Paris to be less overtly racist than the United States – although, as Baldwin pointed out, the Algerians, who were denied civil rights, were the African Americans of France.

Baldwin arrived in Paris the year after the publication in that city of the first issue of *Présence Africaine*, the quarterly cultural, political and literary magazine founded by Alioune Diop. The magazine, formed shortly after the end of the Second World War, was billed as 'open to all contributors of good will (White, Yellow or Black) who might be able to help define African originality and to hasten its introduction into the modern world'. The journal attracted the attention of prominent French intellectuals, including Jean-Paul Sartre, Albert Camus and André Gide, quickly becoming the cultural embodiment of Pan-Africanism, which aimed to foster unity and collaboration among people of African descent.

Richard Wright, Baldwin's former mentor, also engaged enthusiastically with the new journal. After moving to Paris in 1946, he continued to write fiction but his novels published in the 1950s – *The Outsider*, *Savage Holiday* and *The Long Dream* – were critical and commercial failures, eclipsed by his more acclaimed collections of travel writing and reportage. Such works included *Black Power: A Record of Reactions in a Land of Pathos*, an ethnographic study of the Gold Coast on the eve of independence, and *The Color Curtain: A Report on the Bandung Conference*, an account of the meeting of political leaders from twenty-nine decolonising nations across Africa and Asia in Bandung, Indonesia, in 1955.

In contrast to the expansive nature of Wright's non-fiction writing, which explored the political and cultural potential of the Black diaspora, Baldwin's writing remained rooted to the country of his birth. And when he turned his attention to the kinds of Black internationalism in Paris championed by Diop, he wrote as a critical observer rather than participant. In his recollections of the French capital, Paris is depicted as a place of loneliness and isolation, where encounters between expatriate Black Americans dredge up 'past humiliations' from the United States. In contrast to Diop's celebration of Black unity, Baldwin depicts a different reality, in which Black Americans live in 'deliberate' isolation in the French capital.[21] Rather than embracing Pan-Africanism, Baldwin remained sceptical about the possibility of collaboration and communication across different cultures. In his essay 'Encounter on the Seine', Baldwin is at pains to point out the cultural and linguistic differences that separate the African American from Black students from the French colonies. 'They face each other, the Negro and the African', Baldwin writes, 'over a gulf of three hundred years – an alienation too vast to be conquered in an evening's good-will, too heavy and too double-edged ever to be trapped in speech'.[22] In an interview published in 1960 about his encounters with Africans, Baldwin repeatedly says that they 'frightened him', adding that perhaps they 'disgusted me'. 'Whenever I was with an African, we would both be uneasy', he explained. 'On what level to talk? The terms of our life were so different, we almost needed a dictionary to talk...'.[23]

Baldwin's cautious, even wary, views on transnational interchange are illustrated by his essay 'Princes and Powers', his report of the first International Congress of Black Writers and Artists at the Sorbonne in Paris, 1956. The Congress, organised by Diop and others, was a historical gathering of artists and writers and international luminaries that included attendees from the Caribbean and Africa, as well as African Americans. Billed as having the ambitious aim of discussing and establishing the international future and legacy of Black political and artistic production, the Congress was a high-profile event. In his role as reporter, rather than participant, Baldwin cast a critical eye over the proceedings, which included contributions from other Black American artists, among them Wright, Mercer Cook, an educator and later ambassador, and John Davis, a professor and director of the CIA-funded American Information Committee on Race and Caste. If the Congress aimed to unify people of African descent, Baldwin was quick to point out their inescapable differences. The Nigerian poet E. L. Lasebikan, who speaks an 'extremely strange language', Baldwin writes, was 'dressed in a most arresting costume'. Baldwin adds that 'he was wearing a very subdued but very ornately figured silk robe, which looked Chinese, and he wore a red velvet toque, a sign, someone told me that he was a Mohammedan'.[24] Not only does Baldwin's description position him as a Western observer, but his rhetoric is reminiscent of colonial writing about Africa. Baldwin makes no attempt to understand Lasebikan's national dress, described here as a 'costume', and he erroneously identifies the poet's language as 'Youriba' rather than 'Yoruba'.[25]

For Baldwin, rather than unifying the gathered artists of African descent, the Congress in fact illustrated 'that gulf which yawns between the American Negro and all other men of color'.[26] 'For what, beyond the fact that all black men at one time or another left Africa, or have remained there', Baldwin asked, 'do they really have in common?'[27] At one point, Baldwin concedes that people of African descent did have something in common, though again he draws attention to the inexpressibility of this relationship. Baldwin muses on what he describes as Black people's 'precarious ... unutterably painful relation to the white world'.[28] This was a comment that he would later revisit. In an interview eight years after the 1956 Congress, he noted that he 'profoundly distrust[ed]' Négritude, a literary movement that took place between the 1930s and 1950s, and that started among Francophone intellectuals and writers who protested against French colonial rule and the policy of assimilation. For Baldwin,

> oppressions do not necessarily unify so many millions of people all over the world ... 'how in the world is this going to connect to so many different experiences?' To be born in Jamaica, Barbados, or Portugal, or New York, or to be black, wouldn't seem to me to be enough ... and the situation of a man in Jamaica is not the situation of a man in Harlem at all.[29]

According to one of Baldwin's biographers, he was 'frankly skeptical of the interest among American blacks at the time in their African "homeland"'.[30] In a letter, Baldwin observed that 'Africa has been black a long time but American Negroes did not identify themselves with Africa until Africa became identified with power'.[31]

~~~~~

Baldwin left New York aged twenty-four as a promising book reviewer for publications such as *New Leader*, then a liberal anti-Communist publication, and *Commentary*, a magazine aimed at anti-Stalinist Jewish intellectuals. Within a year of his arrival in Paris, he was starting to establish a reputation as a sharp and sensitive essayist. His first novel, which he had begun in New York City, accompanied Baldwin to cheap hotels across Paris. In 1951, he was suffering from a protracted bout of depression and he could not finish his debut novel. Shorter pieces, including the short story 'The Death of the Prophet', were rolling off his typewriter; he wrote several pieces for *The Reporter*, a prominent US anti-fascist magazine, including 'The Negro in Paris' and a substantial review essay titled 'The Negro at Home and Abroad' – but his first novel resisted completion. Emotional and financial support came in the form of Mary Painter, an economist at the American embassy in Paris, who remained his closest female friend, and the teenaged Lucien Happersberger, who had run away from his safe hometown in Lausanne to experience the excitement of post-war Paris. The two young men were inseparable. Baldwin encouraged Happersberger to paint, while his younger friend encouraged him to write. Both men were in love with one another, but in different ways. 'He had a dream of settling down', Happersberger recalled, whose relationship with Baldwin, which lasted

over forty years, began as something sexual but became
fraternal.[32] When I wrote to Monsieur Happersberger in the
early 2000s, his quiet charisma oozed from his beautifully
crafted letter. He recalled his old friend with warmth and
love, but he expressed frustration at the way in which he was
labelled Baldwin's lover, a feature of their relationship that
dwindled early as their deep love changed over their forty-
year relationship.

Aware that Baldwin needed to leave the bustle of
Paris – both for his mental state and to cure his writer's
block – Happersberger hustled his father for money by
claiming he had been struck down with tuberculosis. Using
the inveigled money, both men travelled to Switzerland,
where the Happersbergers owned a small house in Loèche-
les-Bains, a village high in the Alps, to the east of Geneva
and to the west of north-west Italy. Some of Baldwin's best
writing came out of this trip to this tiny village. Not only did
he finish his first novel but his descriptions of living in the
snow-capped Alps are among his finest bits of writing. In his
essay 'The Discovery of What It Means to Be an American'
Baldwin reflects on how, devoid of his props in Paris, and
after suffering what he came to realise was a breakdown, he
was able to think deeply about home as he completed his
novel, now appropriately titled *Go Tell It on the Mountain*:
'There, in that absolutely alabaster landscape, armed with
two Bessie Smith records and a typewriter, I began to try to
re-create the life that I had first known as a child...'. As he
listened to the Empress of the Blues, Baldwin recalled that it
was 'her tone and cadence' which 'helped me to dig back to
the way I myself must have spoken when I was a pickaninny,
and to remember the things I had heard and seen and felt'.[33]

In his reflections on living abroad, Baldwin often returned
to a theme that is captured in a short, haunting film made

by the Turkish filmmaker Sedat Pakay. Titled *James Baldwin: From Another Place*, and shot in Istanbul over three days in May 1970, the film catches intimate scenes of the writer in his bedroom. Dressed at moments only in his underwear, Baldwin addresses the camera in a way that underscores the tensions in his life and work, between private self and public persona:

> I suppose that many people do blame me for being out of the States as often as I am. But one can't afford to worry about that.... [And] perhaps only someone who is outside of the States realizes that it's impossible to get out. The American power follows one everywhere.... One sees it better from a distance ... from another place, from another country.

As one biographer put it, 'Like no other existing documentary, the black-and-white film captures the profound paradox of Baldwin's transatlantic vantage point by showing how he both belongs and remains an outsider in the teeming half-European, half-Asian Turkish metropolis'.[34]

Notwithstanding his long sojourns in France and Turkey, most of Baldwin's work confronts his relationship with the United States. While he loved Istanbul, he does not depict or engage with Turkey in his fiction or essays. As he mused in 1960, 'You have to go far away to find out that you never do get far away', adding, 'I couldn't get to know France. The key to my experience was here, in America. Everything I could deal with was here.'[35] Living abroad, Baldwin intuited, accorded him a critical distance from the country of his birth, a distance he desperately needed not only to write but also to find love.

In 'Notes of a Native Son', Baldwin recalls one incident that took place in Trenton, New Jersey, during the summer of 1943, when he was working at Belle Mead Army Service

Forces Depot, the largest of its kind in the United States. The money was good – $80 a week plus overtime – but spending it proved difficult if, like Baldwin, you refused to eat in segregated restaurants. On one particular evening, having seen a film about the German occupation of France – with the beautifully ironic title *This Is Our Land* – Baldwin and a friend visited the American Diner, where, as was customary, they were told 'We don't serve Negroes here'. Baldwin recalls this moment as a turning point in his life, describing how he 'first contracted some dread, chronic disease, the unfailing symptom of which is a kind of blind fever'.[36] Moving amid the white faces in the street, Baldwin entered a fashionable restaurant 'in which I knew not even the intercession of the Virgin would cause me to be served'.[37] Understanding only too well that he would be refused service, Baldwin again requested a hamburger. Knowing that the waitress would not come any closer, he picked up a water mug and flung it at her. It missed, shattering the mirror behind the bar.

The incident at the restaurant showed Baldwin not only that he could have been murdered but that the 'blind fever' inside him meant that he was capable of killing, too, which became one of the reasons he resolved to leave the United States. When he returned to the States to visit the American South for the first time in 1957, it is striking how much of his writing draws attention to the complex entanglements of home and place. In the South, he would become a stranger in the land of his birth, displaced in a 'territory [that is] absolutely hostile and strange', where he felt 'exactly like a foreigner', a description which carries echoes of his writings about Algerians in Paris.[38] The North Africans, Baldwin writes, 'though they spoke French, and had been, in a sense, produced by France, they were not at home in Paris, no more at home than I, though for a different reason', a comment strongly evocative of his first trip to the American South. Arriving back in New York, Baldwin reflects that 'Now, though I was a stranger, I was home'.[39]

If Baldwin felt a sense of home in Istanbul, which sits at the crossroads between East and West, then his experience lies in stark contrast to his reflections of spending his first winter in Loèche-les-Bains, which produced the superlative essay 'Stranger in the Village'. Baldwin reflects on his experience as the first Black person to visit this 'white wilderness' of around 600 people, an Alpine hamlet 4,500 feet above sea level flanked by mountains on all four sides, without a bank, library or cinema, and which seemed untouched by modernity. After several visits to the village, Baldwin reflects that 'I remain as much a stranger today as I was the first day I arrived', his sense of estrangement compounded by the children who shout 'Neger! Neger!' as he walks along the streets.[40]

Just as he riffs on the notion of house across his essays, here Baldwin expands the notion of village. A decade later, the Canadian media theorist Marshall McLuhan coined the term 'global village' to underscore how technology brought people across the world together. In 'Stranger in the Village', Baldwin reminds the reader of his peripheral position in Western culture, illustrated by the Swiss villagers, whose only point of reference is to connect him to the Africans 'saved' by Swiss missionaries. Although the only typewriter in the village is owned by the urbane and cultured Baldwin, he nonetheless acknowledges that even the illiterate villagers are 'related, in a way that I am not, to Dante, Shakespeare, Michelangelo, Aeschylus, Da Vinci, Rembrandt, and Racine; the cathedral at Chartres says something to them which it cannot say to me...'.[41]

By the late 1960s, as younger writers and activists championed Black Power, a middle-aged Baldwin found himself once more without a seat at the table. Whereas he is now frequently championed as an intersectional hero – one whose Blackness and queerness challenge what are sometimes called heteronormative white power structures – those very positions rendered him an outsider to Black radicalism, at least in some circles, where he was known as 'Martin Luther Queen'. In a discussion of 'Stranger in the Village', Addison Gayle Jr., one of the architects of the Black Arts Movement – the cultural wing of the Black Power Movement – complained of the 'tone of assimilation' in Baldwin's essay, lambasting 'the obsession with fusing the black and white cultures', to the point that he accused Baldwin of 'obliterating racial characteristics altogether'.[42]

Gayle's critique of Baldwin, however, misses the nuances at play in the writer's work. In one of Baldwin's earliest essays, he notes 'that the most crucial time in my own development came when I was forced to recognize that I was a kind of bastard of the West', explaining that this position as an 'interloper' gave him a 'special attitude' when it came to understanding Western culture, including Shakespeare, Bach, Rembrandt and Chartres.[43] 'Stranger in the Village' concludes with the prophetic line, penned not long before countries in Africa started to gain independence: 'This world is white no longer, and will never be white again'.[44] As Baldwin explained thirty years later, in an interview with *Paris Review*:

> Europe is no longer a frame of reference, a standard-bearer, the classic model for literature and for civilization.... When I was a kid the world was white, for all intents and purposes, and now it is struggling to remain white – a very different thing.[45]

~~~

In December 2017, I suggested to my wife that we take a romantic trip across the Alps from where we were staying in the Jura, just north of the Western Alps. Since I don't drive, she took a little persuading, but she acquiesced when I told her about the scenic hotel that I had booked next to thermal hot springs. During the three-hour journey, I read aloud 'Stranger in the Village' and then confessed my main reason for our weekend away. (Baldwin has for some time been the third person in our relationship.) On the approach to Loèche-les-Bains, the roads double back on themselves, contorting like livid scars on the hard mountain rock. Passing through Albinen – the village described by Baldwin as the nearest place with a bank or cinema, I tuned into a crackling local jazz station, and we listened to Bessie Smith sing 'Haunted House Blues'. As we arrived in Loèche-les-Bains, my heart soared as I tried to locate buildings that Baldwin describes in his essay. I had seen footage of the village from an early Pierre Koralnik film. A few years before the musical *Anna*, starring Anna Karina, and the ubiquitous Serge Gainsbourg, he made a short film called *Un étranger dans le village*, which follows Baldwin's return to the Swiss village a decade later, as he narrates his famous essay in somewhat strained French.

Wandering through the narrow streets dotted with chalets, I sensed the thrill of locating buildings that Baldwin describes, an excitement that my wife understood. She grew up at Allan Bank, home to the Wordsworth family between 1808 and 1811, the only house where the poet lived with all three of his children. She inhabited what was then the spare room set aside for Samuel Coleridge, who no doubt slept soundly after his twelve-mile 'circumcursion' from Greta Hall in Keswick. Allan Bank, which has been owned by the National Trust for a hundred years, has commanding views of Lake Grasmere, but was decried as a 'temple of abomination' by Wordsworth. The gardens were a different matter. My wife claims that she can locate the exact spot where the poet composed his verse in the gardens of Allan Bank; she has noticed a shift in poetic style brought on, she argues, by his time at the Georgian villa.

Within half an hour of wandering around Loèche-les-Bains, we identified a building called Ballet Haus, mentioned in Baldwin's essay, and now a ski-hire shop. (Baldwin recalled how the villagers invited him to join them on the slopes 'because they cannot imagine what I look like on skis'.) We entered the small Catholic church where the villagers in Baldwin's time had donated money to save 'the souls of black folks'. The collection box decorated with a black figurine that he describes is no longer on display, but it seems the gold-baroque interior has barely changed.

I enquired about Baldwin, chatting in my halting French to the proprietors of cafés and bars, one of whom thought I was asking about James Bond. Another understood me to be talking about Alec Baldwin. That evening, however, we struck up a conservation with a local woman whose grandmother lives next door to the Happersbergers' family chalet, and she directed us towards the modest house nestled behind Haus Goethe – so named after an earlier literary visitor. (Mark Twain also visited the village in 1878, hot on the heels of Guy de Maupassant, who had stayed the year before.)

As I stood on the ancient flagstones of the steps leading up to Lucien Happersberger's chalet, I felt a sense of intimacy, a notion of shared experience: the source of Baldwin's inspiration was in front of me. For a brief moment that seemed to transcend time, I looked as though through the writer's eyes. In the car, we had listened as Bessie sang 'This house is so haunted with dead men' and here, however irrationally, I felt closer to the writer whom I've been stalking for decades.

I am not alone in wanting to visit these haunted places, which the French historian Pierre Nora, a leading figure in the field of memory studies, has called 'lieux de mémoire', or sites of memory – places or objects which hold memories. For Nora, the past is a contested space between memory and history in which the former is organic and natural, while the latter is a reconstruction of the former, an intellectual process played out across the academy. Nora has a point, particularly when he opines that, if we could truly remember, there would be no need for memorials. Sites of memory, in Nora's schema, are not only conventional memorials, such as First World War monuments, but also sites – both physical and cultural – around which communal memories gather and disperse. For Nora, these 'lieux de mémoire' are places, much like Baldwin's house – and indeed his legacy – in which 'the ultimate embodiments of a memorial consciousness ... [have] barely survived in a historical age'.[46]

Nora may be onto something: visitors flock to Ernest Hemingway's house in Key West, Florida, eager to take in the atmosphere and to spot the descendants of his white polydactyl cat, which roam the grounds. Spend a weekend in Sussex and you can visit the former homes of Virginia Woolf, Henry James and Rudyard Kipling. Writers are not immune to this fascination. Vikram Seth bought the rectory that once belonged to the Anglican poet George Herbert. Allen Ginsberg, overwhelmed at approaching the birthplace of his hero, arrived 'enchanted in England / Weeping at the Foggy earth of England's Blake'.[47]

As we sat in a restaurant near where Baldwin had stayed, mulling over what we had experienced, it struck me how important it is for me to share these moments. Unlike the solitary pleasure of reading, literary pilgrimages can bring fleeting moments of communal joy. But it isn't really possible to see through Baldwin's all-seeing eyes, which never seemed to blink, or to re-create what he felt as the first Black man in this small Swiss village. In our twenty-first-century travellers' luxury, blending in with the mostly white locals, we passed through Loèche-les-Bains without much more than a glance; Baldwin, as the first Black man encountered by the villagers, was 'simply a living wonder'.

As we checked out of our hotel, I thanked the owner, who asked why we had come to the village. Smiling at my response, he led me downstairs to the restaurant, where the paintings of his old friend Lucien Happersberger adorned the walls. We left the dining room, crowded with Lucien's paintings of chalets in snow, and stepped into the blinding sunlight refracted by the ice-tipped mountains.

~~~~~

When he described his legacy as leaving fragments among the ruins, I imagine Baldwin, who was an admirer of T. S. Eliot, was thinking of something more poetic than what has become the waste land of his last home. After he died intestate in 1987, it transpired that he did not legally own his home in St-Paul de Vence that featured in *Architectural Digest*. Campaigners, believing that Baldwin wished to leave his home as a writers' colony, have been battling to save the seventeenth-century house, which had been sold to developers. The project is not without precedent. The childhood home of Nina Simone in Tryon, North California, has been granted status by the National Trust for Historic Preservation, but Baldwin's home in the Côte d'Azur has now been razed.

In 2014, my wife took me to St-Paul de Vence to celebrate my fortieth birthday. The charming mediaeval commune is famous for its art galleries and for the painters, including Matisse, Braque and Miró, who were drawn to the clear mountain light. My interest was of course in Baldwin's connection to the village. We stayed at La Colombe d'Or, a charming family-run hotel and restaurant in which Picasso, Modigliani and of course Baldwin ate, drank and debated. When painters could not afford to pay for their board and lodging, they offered up their artwork in lieu of francs, which explains the establishment's stunning collection. (Meander down the corridors and you'll realise that you're brushing past a picture by Chagall or Kandinsky.) In the terraced bar, I spoke to several people who knew the writer well. One of the waiters had lodged with Baldwin for a few months in the early 1980s. He remembered his kindness, recalling that he was frequently invited to join Baldwin and his guests for dinner on the terrace. I spoke to a woman whose mother had worked at La Colombe d'Or, where Baldwin had been a familiar figure. 'He was ugly in a way', she told me, but 'he could seduce anyone'. Others recalled his charisma and his infectious laughter.

On the morning of my birthday, I went in search of Baldwin's house, which took me some time as I have a patho-logical inability to listen to directions. A local man explained that it was abandoned and that there were rumours that the house was going to be knocked down and that plans for holiday homes were afoot. The doorbell wires had been pulled out and the rusty padlock confirmed that nobody lived there. I hopped – nimbly I like to think – over the wall. As my feet hit the scorched grass on what used to be several acres of olive trees, cypress pines and lavender, I felt exhilara-tion, but also sadness. To my left was a crumbling gatehouse where Baldwin's old assistant, Bernard Hassell, had lived. A friend from the early Paris days, Hassell, a charismatic dancer, helped Baldwin run the house. I stepped over shards of broken glass strewn across dull dry floorboards. I peered inside one cupboard and found a row of solitary hooks which once held keys to the main house.

I walked through an overgrown terrace, but I could not locate 'the welcome table' where Baldwin entertained his guests, among them Josephine Baker and Miles Davis. At the back of the house, a new plywood door had 'W.C.' scrawled in chalk, evidence, I supposed of the renovation project. At the back of the house, I found broken shutters and open windows connecting several downstairs rooms, including what looked like an old stable with a stone water trough. As I wandered through the house, I recognised the fireplace from the *Architectural Digest* piece which pictured Baldwin's study – or 'torture chamber' as he sometimes called it. 'You don't live where you're happy', he wrote to the editor Sol Stein, 'you do your best to live where you work'.[48]

It was difficult to reconcile the bare rooms of Baldwin's study with a picture I had seen of him at work, which showed a painting by his old friend Beauford Delaney, a drink – probably Johnnie Walker Black Label – a sheath of papers and an exhausted-looking typewriter. I searched in vain for some sign that he had worked here, which I knew was unlikely. After his death in 1987, his brother David moved in, and he and Bernard Hassell remained there until their respective deaths. In the garden, I spotted a pitchfork, which I doubt that Baldwin used, although he was fond of quoting the final line of Voltaire's *Candide*, 'il faut cultiver notre jardin'. During Baldwin's time at the house, the garden was an arcadia of almond and peach trees, but on my visit it was little more than brambles and thorns. Just as I was about to leave, I spotted a small orange tree, which, smothered by grass and weeds, against the odds still bore fruit. I thought of Tony Harrison's poem 'A Kumquat for John Keats', in which the speaker of the poem, who is, like me, 'a man of doubt at life's mid-way', imagines the Romantic poet eating 'this Eastern citrus scarcely cherry size'. After his first bite of kumquat, Harrison's speaker describes Keats's experience as 'History, a life, the heart, the brain / flow to the taste buds and flow back again'. As I tore into the sagging peel and bit through the tough white pith, I tasted a strange but not quite bitter fruit.[49]

As we returned to La Colombe d'Or for my birthday dinner, one of the waiters who had remembered Baldwin told me that I was sitting at his favourite table. He had been a frequent visitor to the restaurant, where he drank, debated and laughed in the balmy summer evenings. Our final evening in St-Paul de Vence lasted through the night and into the wee small hours. I bought drinks for everyone present to celebrate my birthday, buoyed by the excitement of visiting Baldwin's home. (Years later, my wife told me that I had racked up a bar bill of nearly 700 euros, a detail she chose not to mention at the time.)

Why is it so important to preserve Baldwin's homes and to set foot in the places that he lived and worked? There's the thrill of walking down a street that he must have trod; and there's the excitement about visiting places that Baldwin wrote about in his work: a sense of being closer to the writer, of sharing an experience and a moment. There's also a danger that visitors to places inhabited by Baldwin will experience the frisson of, say, drinking in a bar that he frequented, but they will leave without any greater understanding of his life and work – just as Baldwin critiqued protest fiction, which claims to effect change but rarely engenders action. The protest novel, Baldwin points out, 'so far from being disturbing, is an accepted and comforting aspect of the American scene, ramifying that framework we believe to be necessary'.[50] There's an implicit assumption that readers of Baldwin's work who seek out his scattered papers across different archives and visit the sites of his various homes can amass these details to finally assemble what the scholar D. Quentin Miller has called the 'half-finished jigsaw puzzle' of the writer's life and work.[51] Paying attention to the environments that produced Baldwin may teach us more about his life and work, but it will require time and effort – and much more than a day trip to the south of France or Switzerland. For white writers, including myself, it is simply not possible to understand how Baldwin felt as the first Black visitor to that tiny Swiss village.

Baldwin's declaration in *Giovanni's Room* that home is 'perhaps ... not a place but simply an irrecoverable condition' is far from straightforward.[52] With brutal economy, he picks apart the differences between home and place and suggests that neither is concerned with geographical space. Home, he suggests, is a condition which cannot be changed; it is metaphysical, rather than geographical. 'There's no place like home' the narrator of Baldwin's short story 'This Morning, This Evening, So Soon' hears a passenger declare as they arrive by boat in New York. Baldwin's writing suggests, rather, that there is no place that *is* home.[53] In his essays and fiction, home is frequently invoked to describe an interior space, where the writer meditates on what it means to be at home in the world. It's a condition sometimes called interiority or, as Baldwin might have called it, the mysterious self. But, as Baldwin reminds us, there is journeying to be undertaken in order to reach this place: 'Go back to where you started, or as far back as you can, examine all of it, travel your road again and tell the truth about it. Sing or shout or testify or keep it to yourself: but *know whence you came.*'[54]

~~~~~

I wish I had asked my father where he thought he was from. Born in Cheshire, where his father happened to be briefly stationed during the late years of the Second World War, his home changed countries every three years. I wish we had spoken more about Baldwin's meditations on home and place. 'You don't have a home until you leave it', Giovanni tells David in Baldwin's second novel, 'and then, when you have left it, you never can go back'.[55] If home is 'at the heart of the real', as the Romanian philosopher Mircea Eliade put it, then this beautiful-sounding concept is complicated when the real becomes unknown, where the past is not just another country but an unfamiliar one.[56] Towards the end of his life, Ralph Waldo Emerson, probably suffering from dementia, acknowledged that 'My memory hides itself', to the point that he began to believe that he was a visitor in someone else's home.[57] 'Without a home at the center of the real', as John Berger points out, 'one was not only shelterless but also lost in nonbeing, in unreality'.[58] As he lives out his final days in a care home, a place he will not leave until he dies, my father no longer knows whence he came, or where he is going. At the still point of a turning world, he has arrived too early at the banks of Lethe.

Chapter 3

Some who wander are lost

I am saying that a journey is called that because you cannot know what you will discover on the journey, what you will do with what you find, or what you find will do to you.

James Baldwin, *I Am Not Your Negro* (2016)

On 18 February 1965, my father had recently turned twenty-one. He was living in Cambridge, where he was studying English literature at Fitzwilliam House, a small college which had been established in the nineteenth century for students, like my grandmother, who did not have the financial means to study at university. The musician Nick Drake arrived at what was by then called Fitzwilliam College two years after my father, who in turn recalled playing football with Eric 'Bone' Idle, later of Monty Python fame, whom he knew slightly from performing in the Footlights.

My father read voraciously during his degree, but often his books of choice bore no connection to the course he was taking, a hint of his gentle iconoclasm. He told me that during the mid-1960s he had attended a demonstration in London dressed in a tweed suit. When one of his peers had mocked him for dressing as part of the Establishment, my father had pointed out that he was the only besuited demonstrator amid hundreds of young people in jeans. He had a point: around the same time, the *Paris Review* interviewed William S. Burroughs, the heroin-chasing architect of the Beat Generation, who was a fastidious dresser. The interviewer, the wonderfully named Conrad Knickerbocker, noted that Burroughs 'might have been a senior partner in a private bank, charting the course of huge but anonymous fortunes'.[1] In footage of Burroughs caught in London during the late 1960s, the author of *Naked Lunch* chastises his bearded and long-haired acolytes: 'I'm urging you all to shave off your beards and dress as I do', Burroughs told his young audience, 'and therefore be a real underground'.[2]

Richard Field shared little else with Burroughs, but both men forged their own respective paths. My father recalled how he and some of his undergraduate friends wore a green carnation in their jacket lapels as a nod to their hero, Oscar Wilde. During his undergraduate days, a family friend once told me, my father was drawn to both men and women, although, like Baldwin, he saw no need for labels such as bisexual. 'Never assume you're heterosexual', my father told me in my teens.

I have no way of knowing why, on 18 February 1965, my father attended one of the most famous Cambridge Union debates of the twentieth century, in which Baldwin battled with the conservative intellectual William F. Buckley Jr. Perhaps my father had been reading *The Fire Next Time* (1963) one of the manifestos of the Civil Rights Movement, instead of thinking about his undergraduate exams. Or perhaps he had picked up a copy of *Another Country* (1962), a novel which sold well but which divided critics, who were uncertain how to read the captivating but sprawling story that recounted interracial and bisexual relationships in New York City. It's very unlikely that Baldwin would have been on the Cambridge English literature curriculum. The scholar and latterly filmmaker Henry Louis Gates Jr. recalled studying for his doctorate at Clare College, Cambridge, during the mid-1970s. When he told his tutor that he was planning to write his thesis on Black literature, his tutor's disdain was evident. 'Tell me, sir ... what is "black" literature?'[3] Perhaps a friend suggested to my father that they should hear Baldwin speak; after all, he had become a leading voice of the Civil Rights Movement by the mid-1960s, which might explain why the hall was full beyond its official capacity. I have looked for my father in the footage of the debate, which was filmed by the BBC, but I can't spot him. There's one frame, a third of the way into the film, in which I thought, just for a moment, he appeared – but as I paused and scrutinised the screen, the figure disappeared from the camera's focus, just as I have disappeared from his purview.

Baldwin's presence at Cambridge drew attention to the battle for civil rights across the Atlantic, but in February 1965 Britain was still six months away from passing the Race Relations Act, an ineffectual piece of legislation which sought to prohibit discrimination on racial grounds in 'places of public resort', meaning that it effectively sanctioned prejudice for private landlords. A year before the Cambridge debate, Peter Griffiths, the Conservative Member of Parliament for Smethwick, a town north-west of Birmingham, had been elected on the back of the slogan 'If you want a nigger for a neighbour, vote Labour'. When asked whether he would double down on his inflammatory shibboleth, Griffiths claimed that it was 'a manifestation of popular feeling'.[4]

A few months before the Baldwin–Buckley debate, Malcolm X – who was by then going by his new Muslim name, El-Hajj Malik El-Shabazz – had spoken at Oxford University's 'Queen and Country' Union debate, an event which had been well attended by a crowd of students, of whom an overwhelming majority were white, who were quick to condemn the racial inequities in the United States but who took longer to open their eyes to the discrimination around them. When El-Shabazz visited Smethwick nine days before he was cut down by bullets in New York, he was taken to the Blue Gates public house, which had a separate bar for Black and Asian patrons. Entering the whites-only smoke room, the Civil Rights activist was refused service, a stark reminder that the Black freedom struggle stretched from Birmingham, Alabama, to Birmingham in the West Midlands of England.

Buckley, Baldwin's debating opponent, was a suave smooth-talker, described by Norman Mailer as 'the leading young Conservative in the [United States], and in fact the most important Conservative in the public eye after Barry Goldwater'.[5] Born fifteen months apart in New York City, both Baldwin and Buckley were around forty years old at the time of the debate, but the Harlem-born writer edged it when it came to international prominence. He was in the United Kingdom principally to help promote the paperback edition of *Another Country*, a plan hatched by his agent, Robert Lantz, and representatives at the Corgi publishing house. Buckley, whose privileged upbringing was the polar opposite of Baldwin's impoverished childhood, had a patrician confidence that he honed at Yale University, the alma mater that he chastised in his first book, *God and Man at Yale*, for not having impressed upon its alumni the importance of individualism, capitalism and Christianity. His next book, a defence of Senator Joseph McCarthy, established an effective brand of conservatism based on anti-Communism, free-market capitalism and moral and political traditionalism. By the time he was thirty, he had founded *National Review*, a magazine devoted to expanding American conservatism as the Civil Rights Movement was taking off in the mid-1950s.

Buckley had a knack for raising funds for projects, but financial help was close to home. His father, William F. Buckley Sr., whose wealth was gained through law and oil, gave his son, when still a young man, around $750,000 in today's money. In 1965, Buckley unsuccessfully ran for mayor of New York City, pre-empting Mailer's disastrous campaign by four years. The following year, he started hosting *Firing Line*, a public-affairs television programme which he went on to anchor for thirty-three years. Guests ranged from an inebriated Jack Kerouac to a seething Noam Chomsky and a smiling Mother Teresa. Though usually polite, Buckley was not averse to *ad hominem* snipes, the most famous of which occurred in a debate with the writer Gore Vidal for ABC News. Following a heated exchange about the Chicago Democratic National Convention of 1968, at which over 2,000 people were arrested for protesting against the Vietnam War, the writers nearly came to blows. Buckley called Vidal – the author of *The City and the Pillar*, the first mainstream American novel about homosexuality – 'queer' and threatened to punch him after his guest described him as a 'pro- or crypto-Nazi'.[6]

In 1957, Buckley penned an infamous editorial for the *National Review*, 'Why the South Must Prevail', which insisted that whites were the most 'advanced' race and were therefore more suited to govern. 'It is not easy, and it is unpleasant, to adduce statistics evidencing the median cultural superiority of White over Negro', Buckley noted, but he managed to do so nonetheless in an article that contrasted Black American 'backwardness' against white Southern 'civilized standards'. Remarkably, Buckley claimed that white Southerners were 'entitled' to rule the South, regardless of how people voted in local elections.[7] Buckley's incendiary remarks carried echoes of those of William Faulkner, author of *The Sound and the Fury* and *As I Lay Dying*. Seven years after receiving the Nobel Prize for Literature, the Mississippian had become increasingly alarmed by the pace of racial desegregation in the South. In an interview with Russell Warren Howe, New York correspondent to the London *Sunday Times*, an inebriated Faulkner famously declared, 'As long as there is a middle road, all right, I'll be on it. But if it came to fighting I'd fight for Mississippi against the United States even if it meant going out into the street and shooting Negroes'.[8]

In a short editorial titled 'Voices of Sanity', Buckley defended Faulkner's views, arguing that the writer's scepticism about the desegregation of schooling was a political, not racial, position, a view not shared by Baldwin. In an essay for *Partisan Review*, a leading cultural, political and literary magazine, Baldwin insisted that Faulkner's comments must be taken seriously, framing them within a penetrating discussion of Northern and Southern moral identities. Acknowledging that Faulkner, like much of the South, was clinging onto a deep-seated notion of tradition that included a belief in racial superiority, Baldwin – in what could also have been a rebuttal to 'Why the South Must Prevail' – wrote that 'Any real change implies the breakup of the world as one has always known it, the loss of all that gave one an identity, the end of safety'.[9] In Buckley's conservative schema, the traditions of the white South needed to be defended, a position which, he claimed, much like his defence of Faulkner, was political, not moral. For Baldwin, such a question was inextricably bound to questions of morality. And in sharp contrast to his debating adversary at Cambridge, Baldwin wanted to smash the very frames of reference that Buckley sought to uphold. As he explained in an open letter to his nephew, 'the black man has functioned in the white man's world as a fixed star, as an immovable pillar', but this was starting to change as the Civil Rights Movement gathered momentum.[10] Innocent people – often a shorthand in Baldwin's writing for white people, and especially white Southerners – are 'still trapped in a history which they do not understand', he declared, 'and until they understand it, they cannot be released from it'.[11]

By 1965, Baldwin had emerged as the most important American writer of the Civil Rights Movement, while Buckley was fast becoming the most visible conservative figure of his generation. As one political scientist puts it, 'At the heart of that message was the belief that American society was basically good, and that it was the sacred duty of conservatives to defend it from any ideas, personalities, or movements that were deemed threats to it'.[12]

At Cambridge, the stage was set for the two eloquent orators, one from an impoverished Harlem background with no university education and the other hailing from a privileged milieu where an Ivy League education was a rite of passage. Baldwin had honed his oratorical skills as a teenage preacher in storefront Pentecostal churches, while Buckley's magniloquence was hewn from dinner parties and the Yale Debate Association.

The motion of the debate – 'The American Dream is at the expense of the American Negro' – selected with Baldwin's writing in mind, was a surprisingly forward-thinking idea put forward by a university renowned for its conservatism. Or, to put it another way, the vast majority of the students at Cambridge had no need for the equivalent of the American Dream, since they hailed from the upper echelons of society. Along with 'Manifest Destiny', the mid- to late-nineteenth-century belief in the divinely ordained right of the United

States to expand its territory, the American Dream has been part of the country's mythos for nearly 100 years, ever since it became popularised by the historian James Truslow Adams in *The Epic of America*. Written as the Great Depression of the 1930s was taking hold – a period in which many Americans began to question the unequal distribution of wealth – Adams began by painting a picture of the American Dream that was less to do with monetary success and more about social equality. In the preface to his Pulitzer Prize-winning book, the former investment banker, who had enjoyed a gilded youth among Brooklyn's social elite, declared that the 'American dream of a better, richer, and happier life for all our citizens of every rank ... is the greatest contribution we have as yet made to the thought and welfare of the world'.[13]

By the mid-1960s, Adams' notions of the American Dream had been repurposed. During the 1950s, it had become increasingly synonymous with seemingly insatiable consumers who were beguiled by sophisticated new methods of television advertising. The 1960s, as depicted in the television series *Mad Men* (2007–15), became a golden age of advertising, when television replaced radio as the most effective medium to entice consumers into buying what they desired but did not need. In *The Hidden Persuaders*, a popular book first published in 1957 that demystified the advertising techniques of the times, the author, Vance Packard, claimed that television was in fact produced to increase advertising space, rather than the other way around. In *The Dharma Bums*, Jack Kerouac's follow-up to *On the Road*, the narrator observes that most Americans in the 1950s are 'imprisoned in a system of work, produce, consume, work, produce, consume'.[14]

The shift in the American Dream from Adams' treatise on liberal democracy to a focus on individual wealth tells only one part of the story. Missing from Adams' thesis on the American Dream is any acknowledgement of how Black Americans fit into 'a dream of a social order in which each man and each woman shall be able to attain to the fullest stature of which they are innately capable, and be recognized by others for what they are, regardless of the fortuitous circumstances of birth or position'.[15] In the early 1950s, the Black American poet Langston Hughes asked 'What happens to a dream deferred?', wondering whether it festers, withers or explodes.[16] Sixty years later, in *Between the World and Me* (2015), Ta-Nehisi Coates began his book with a letter to his teenaged son, an echo of Baldwin's letter to his nephew in *The Fire Next Time*. Like Baldwin, who counsels that Americans 'do not dare to examine' the American Dream and 'are far from having made it a reality', Coates dismisses the notion of equality in US society.[17] He recalls that 'for so long [he] ... wanted to escape into the Dream' but he eventually realised that had 'never been an option'.[18] While the Declaration of Independence states that 'Life, Liberty, and the pursuit of Happiness' are Americans' 'unalienable Rights', Coates calls out the myth of the United States of America as a country built on the foundations of freedom and equality.

Baldwin, like Hughes before him and Coates after him, exposes the dangerous fiction of what he calls in 'Everybody's Protest Novel' 'the sunlit prison of the American dream' and 'fantasies, connecting nowhere with reality, sentimental'.[19] As he put it a few years before his clash with Buckley, the American Dream had 'therefore become something much more closely resembling a nightmare, on the private, domestic, and international levels'.[20] African Americans, Baldwin had cautioned in *The Fire Next Time*, 'may never be able to rise to power, but they are very well placed indeed to precipitate chaos and bring down the curtain on the American dream'.[21] In an essay published shortly after his debate with

Buckley, Baldwin stated, 'Unless we can establish some kind of dialogue between those people who enjoy the American dream and those people who have not achieved it, we will be in terrible trouble'.[22]

On Thursday 18 February 1965, Baldwin and Buckley both arrived in Cambridge, Buckley in a black Austin limousine, Baldwin in what the president of the Union described as the 'gaudiest limousine I had ever seen'.[23] Buckley was greeted at the Union by friends, including the actor James Mason, while Baldwin, ignoring the directive to wear black tie, arrived with his entourage in a blue suit with a red tie. Crash barriers had been put in place in an attempt to stop students from spilling over from the hall, which had quickly filled. 'There are undergraduates everywhere', the BBC commentator announced (presumably in sharp contrast to some of the lecture halls), 'they're on the benches, they're on the floor, they're in the galleries and there are a lot more outside clamouring to get in'.[24]

Baldwin was the third speaker at the debate, following the tradition at the Cambridge Union in which the undergraduate proposer of the debate is followed by the opposer. The opposer of the motion was a South African student called Jeremy Burford, who claimed that the American Dream had in fact improved race relations as well as the lot of Black Americans. Drawing on his years as a child preacher, Baldwin announced himself with the line 'I find myself, not for the first time, in the position of a kind of Jeremiah'. Without glancing at his notes, Baldwin described the motion as 'hideously loaded', adding 'one's response to that question – one's reaction to that question – has to depend on ... where you find yourself in the world'.

The last remark was clearly a swipe at Buckley, who had recently returned from a skiing holiday in Switzerland.

Employing his powerful oratorical skills, Baldwin personalised the history of racial oppression: 'I picked the cotton, and I carried it to market, and I built the railroads, under someone else's whip, for nothing. For nothing.' The speech ended in a rapturous standing ovation, an unusual occurrence at Union debates.

Buckley looked to be in a precarious position even before he opened his mouth. But he attacked with an element of surprise by claiming that Baldwin was in fact treated with deference: 'The American community, almost everywhere he goes, treats him with a kind of unction, a kind of satisfaction at posturing carefully before his flagellations of our civilization', a line of attack that built on several pieces in *National Review* in which Baldwin was deemed a tricky adversary. Buckley's tactic was to address his opponent as 'a fellow American', in a way that bypassed any reference to race: 'The fact that you sit here ... and lay the entire weight of the Negro ordeal on your own shoulders is irrelevant to the argument that we are here to discuss'. It was a move that did not work with the assembled student audience, 544 of whom voted in favour of the motion and 164 in favour of Buckley.

Videos of the Baldwin–Buckley debate can be found easily online. The black-and-white footage fizzes with Baldwin's charisma and confirms the writer as the heavyweight champion orator of his generation. During his troubled years as a teenage preacher in Pentecostal churches in Harlem, Baldwin recalled that he 'would improvise from the texts, like a jazz musician improvises from a theme. I never wrote a sermon – I studied the texts. I've never written a speech. I can't read a speech'.[25]

Similarly, during the Cambridge debate, Baldwin did not rely on his notes; he worked the crowd with his inimitable linguistic artistry that conveyed sincerity and experience

with elegance and grace. And while his opponent accused
Baldwin of affecting a British accent during the debate, it
was in fact Buckley's mellifluous drawl that was notably
anglicised, described as 'High Church' and 'mid-Atlantic', a
feature that did not endear him to my father and his friends,
who were mesmerised by Baldwin's magnetism and turned
off by Buckley's self-assurance.

~~~~~~

There's a restlessness about Baldwin that I find appealing,
which cuts across his writing and his life. Early on in his
career as a writer, he made it clear that he did not believe in
categories and that it was impossible to indoctrinate him.
And every time I think I've got Baldwin pegged down, I read
something else by him which makes me rethink my position.
His first novel, *Go Tell It on the Mountain*, is a masterpiece
of late modernist fiction, which recounts one day in the life
of John Grimes, a fourteen-year-old who bears more than a
passing resemblance to his creator. Set in Harlem during the
mid-1930s, the novel announced Baldwin as a major writer
of Black American fiction. He followed this acclaimed novel
with a collection of essays, *Notes of a Native Son*, in which he
cited Charles Dickens, the King James Bible and Henry James
as his major influences. Two of James's novels, *The Portrait
of a Lady* and *The Princess Casamassima*, were listed as books
'that had helped him break out of the ghetto', a detail I have
yet to see on social media, where a rather narrow version of
the author is presented.[26] As he garnered acclaim as a new
voice in African American literature of the 1950s, Baldwin
wrote about escaping 'the "cage" of Negro writing', just as

he insisted on being described as an American, not African American, writer.[27] Notwithstanding the success of his first novel, which was nominated for a National Book Award, Baldwin changed tack. Rather than write another novel about African American life, he published *Giovanni's Room*, a slim novel set in Paris in which there are ostensibly no Black characters. As his career progressed, readers and critics seemed unsure how to place him. Was he an essayist who also wrote fiction, or the other way around? What about his poetry and his plays? Was he a Black writer or a gay writer? Was he a religious writer, or a fierce critic of the church?

In *Go Tell It on the Mountain*, John Grimes has no desire to become a preacher like his stepfather, and most readers will sympathise with a sensitive fourteen-year-old who is unsure about his place in the world, and to whom he is attracted – men, women, or both. At Grimes's home, as was the case in Baldwin's childhood, jazz music and the cinema are forbidden, distractions created by the devil to lead the flock astray. Near the start of the novel, John fantasises about another kind of life, one in which he 'became immediately beautiful, tall, and popular'. Turning his back on the ways of the church, John pictures himself as 'a poet, or a college lecturer president, or a movie star; he drank expensive whisky, and he smoked Lucky Strike cigarettes in the green package'.[28]

Like many first novels, *Go Tell It on the Mountain* is transparently underpinned by autobiographical experience. John Grimes and James Baldwin share many characteristics: both were bright students who were cowed by a disciplinarian and religious stepfather and both dreamt of escaping the church. Baldwin would have made a terrible college lecturer president, but by the 1960s his snappy wardrobe and sunglasses made him look like the celebrity he was fast becoming. He had a penchant for Johnnie Walker whisky and it's hard to find a photograph of him without a cigarette in his hand. (He claimed that he chain-smoked in New York due to the pressure he felt there.)[29] In the short film *James Baldwin: From Another Place*, shot when the writer was forty-five, Baldwin is filmed waking up, getting out of his bed in a pair of white Y-fronts, putting on a short silk dressing gown and lighting a cigarette as he opens the window. Baldwin smokes with such panache that he looks like a movie star from the 1940s, a time when – in films such as *Casablanca* – smoking frequently stood in for sex. Every time I see this clip, I reach for my tobacco, even though I gave up smoking long ago. And while Baldwin wrote two volumes of poetry – only one of which, *Jimmy's Blues*, was published – it was his poetic prose that dazzled, rather than his uneven verse. (When Malcolm X referred to Baldwin as the poet of the revolution, it was unlikely that he was referring to his poems.)

Ernest Hemingway's famous directive on writing insisted that 'Prose is architecture, not interior decoration.... People in a novel ... must be projected from the writer's assimilated experience, from his knowledge, from his head, from his heart and from all that there is of him'.[30] Baldwin, who was an admirer of Hemingway's early writing and whose second novel, *Giovanni's Room*, is indebted to *The Sun Also Rises*, would likely have agreed. 'A great writer operates as an unimpeachable witness to one's own experience', Baldwin wrote, 'and one of the reasons that great writers are so rare (and their careers, in the main, so stormy) is that almost no one wishes to have his experience corroborated'.[31]

Baldwin's drive to communicate his experience, which was both personal and also something that he seemed impelled to share, was at times painful and difficult, and there are instances where life and art are reflected and refracted in uncomfortable ways. His second and final novel of the 1960s,

Tell Me How Long the Train's Been Gone (1968), is the tale of a middle-aged gay Black actor, Leo Proudhammer, who grapples with the tensions between art and activism, a story that Baldwin knew only too well. 'Some people considered me a faggot', Proudhammer acknowledges, 'for some I was a hero, for some I was a whore, for some I was a devious cocksman, for some I was an Uncle Tom', a sentiment to which Baldwin bore witness in his next major publication. In *No Name in the Street*, a searing book-length essay that is driven by his reflection on the Civil Rights Movement and the shift towards Black Power, Baldwin's despair cuts across the pages of his essay as he writes about the assassinations of Medgar Evers, Malcolm X and Martin Luther King Jr. Baldwin knew all three men, who would be the subject of his barely started memoir, *Remember This House*. Some journeys, though, are too difficult to recount; his proposed book remained in note form, its tragic subject matter resisting narrative, and therefore sense.

No Name in the Street is one of Baldwin's most intriguing essays. Written as he approached fifty – with one boot firmly planted in the field of middle age and the other kicking up dirt in a patch of revolutionary soil – it captures what the writer called 'the price of the ticket', the toll it takes to pay one's dues. The title of Baldwin's essay is revealing. On the one hand, in the early 1970s he was still one of the most famous living American authors, but he was becoming less relevant to the younger generation as each year went by. His then most recent novel, *Tell Me How Long the Train's Been Gone*, had been panned by critics, but he was still capable of unparalleled eloquence in interviews. In longer forms, including novels and book-length essays, Baldwin's work showed signs of unevenness, even as his writing remained compelling and at times surprising. *No Name* is an essay that sits at the crossroads of Baldwin's career. Much of it looks back to the hard road of the Civil Rights Movement, which had changed direction by the time the essay was published. Following the assassination of Malcolm X in 1965, an increasing number of activists began to doubt the efficacy of non-violent action, inspired by the Black Panther Party for Self-Defense, which was formed by Bobby Seale and Huey P. Newton in late 1966. Beginning in Oakland, California, the Marxist–Leninist organisation soon spread nationally and attracted thousands of younger African Americans. The shift in activism is highlighted by the career of Stokely Carmichael (Kwame Ture), a charismatic graduate from Howard University in Washington, DC, who spent the early 1960s involved in non-violent protests, including marches, assemblies and sit-ins. In 1966, he coined the term 'Black Power' at a rally in Mississippi, a frequently misunderstood term that in fact represented a call for economic, political and cultural self-determination, as well as an insistence that Blackness should be associated with pride, not shame.

Over the years, Baldwin had made it clear that he did not believe in economic and cultural separatism. In *The Fire Next Time*, he had 'dismissed the Nation of Islam's demand for a separate black economy in America ... as willful, and even mischievous, nonsense'.[32] He ends a gripping account of his audience with Elijah Muhammad, the Nation of Islam leader for more than forty years – and mentor to Malcolm X – with a cheeky comment about leaving to 'have a drink with several white devils on the other side of town'.[33] In his writing and speeches, Baldwin is adamant that the challenge his country of birth faces is not to maintain segregation but to allow people to work and live together, no matter the cost. As Baldwin counselled his nephew at the start of *The Fire Next Time*, 'There is no reason for you to try to become like white people' but 'You must accept them and accept them with love'.[34]

By the time the Black Power Movement was underway, Baldwin's comment about accepting white people with love seemed out of step with his peers, aligning him with Martin Luther King Jr.'s peaceful protests rather than Malcolm X's 'by any means necessary' approach. In an essay published in 1963 – the same year as *The Fire Next Time* – the writer LeRoi Jones, who would shortly change his name to Amiri Baraka, described severing ties with his white friends and preparing for the 'war going on now in the United States'.[35] And to complicate matters, Baldwin's homosexuality, which he refused to keep hidden, was the source of cruel attacks. Towards the end of the 1960s, Eldridge Cleaver, one of the Black Panther leaders, wrote *Soul on Ice*, a collection of essays which, with its blend of personal accounts and political observations, was heavily indebted to Baldwin's writing style but which he used to undermine the older writer. Cleaver wrote disparagingly of Baldwin's 'Martin Luther King-type self-effacing love for his oppressors', a remark that was throat-clearing for some vicious comments to follow.[36] In a disturbing twist, Cleaver justified the rape of white women as an 'insurrectionary' act which avenged slavery, but he described homosexuality as 'a sickness, just as are baby-rape or wanting to become the head of General Motors'.[37]

Baldwin remarked that 'being attacked by white people only made him flare hotly into eloquence; being attacked by black people ... made him want to break down and cry'.[38] In *No Name in the Street*, rather than tackling Cleaver, Baldwin described him as 'valuable and rare' but nevertheless said that the younger writer had confused him with 'the unutterable debasement of the male – with all those faggots, punks, and sissies, the sight and sound of whom, in prison, must have made him vomit more than once'.[39] Baldwin, who had previously made it clear that he was against bloodshed, now aligned himself with his Black Power comrades, claiming that his life had 'more than once depended on the gun in a brother's holster'.[40] In a dramatic shift from accepting white people with love, Baldwin wrote that 'it is not necessary for a black man to hate a white man, or to have any particular feelings about him at all, in order to realize that he must kill him'.[41]

No Name in the Street is riddled with instances in which Baldwin questions his reputation, including (closely mirroring Leo Proudhammer in *Tell Me How Long the Train's Been Gone*) asking 'what in the world was I by now but an aging, lonely, sexually dubious, politically outrageous, unspeakably erratic freak?'[42] On the one hand, Baldwin points out that he had temporarily returned to the United States to participate in the Civil Rights Movement or, as he frequently put it, to bear witness: 'I will always consider myself among the greatly privileged', he writes, 'because, however inadequately, I was there'.[43] But he is also deeply aware that 'the general reaction to famous people who hold difficult opinions is that they can't really mean it'; there is a perception that, as a celebrity writer, he marched in Montgomery merely 'to sell ... books'.[44]

~~~~~

In Baldwin's writing and interviews, travel is at times described as a physical journey, but he also frequently alludes to it as something metaphysical and metaphorical, a philosophical or spiritual passage. When Baldwin stated that 'I don't believe in nations anymore. Those passports, those borders are as outworn and useless as war', it's a position which is in keeping with descriptions of himself as a maverick, someone who questions identity categories and who refuses to be pigeonholed.[45] And when Baldwin wrote to his agent, Jay Acton, to set out his premise for *Remember This House* – the book about Malcolm X, Martin Luther King Jr. and Medgar Evers – the language is not just about travelling back to the American South but also about proceeding down the difficult path of memory:

> This is a journey, to tell you the truth, which I always knew that I would have to make, but had hoped, perhaps (certainly, I had hoped) not to have to make so soon.[46]

In the introduction to *The Price of the Ticket*, a collection of his non-fiction that was published in 1985, two years before his death, Baldwin reflected on his life. While many commentators had assumed that the writer had abandoned his faith early on, his language, hewn from the scriptures, suggests a more complicated relationship with the church. 'To do your first works over', Baldwin wrote, 'means to reexamine everything. Go back to where you started ... examine all of it, travel your road again ... *know whence you came.*'[47]

Re-reading Baldwin's exhortation to 'reexamine everything', I am struck by what this means for people, like my father, who do not know whence they came. I remember my father telling me – when he was around the age that I am now – that he was looking forward to becoming old so that he could sit still and listen to the world around him; that old age would be the perfect time to begin meditation as the body and mind slow down. Part of me takes comfort in the knowledge that my father cannot reflect on his imminent death – which, for me, induces a profound sense of loneliness – but sometimes I feel he has been tricked out of a chance to reflect on his life, to reminisce, to say goodbye, or to make amends. In the poem 'Spirit of '76' by John Updike – a writer whose novels my father devoured – as my father retreats into silence, I am moved by the line 'Be with me, words, a little longer', written as the writer was dying from lung cancer.[48] But in 'Endpoint', the title poem of the volume in which 'Spirit of '76' appears, Updike writes 'Age I must, but die I would rather not', and I am unsure whether to be relieved that my father seems unaware of his fast-diminishing life or aggrieved that he has been robbed of a chance of reflection.[49]

One of the last journeys that my father took was to Norfolk, where his father was from and where my grandfather had courted my grandmother. For twenty years my father had kept in separate urns his parents' ashes, unsure about when or where to scatter them. For a few weeks, my grandmother resided in the front seat of his car. He surprised several people by asking them, as they entered his old Renault, whether they minded if his mother sat on their lap. At one point my grandparents were reunited in the garage, where their urns blended in with jars of chutney and jam.

My youngest sister drove my parents down to Norfolk at a point when my father was wracked with anxiety as his memory flickered and dimmed like an electrical outage. My father, who loved the architecture of churches, found a graveyard that he wanted to visit. When he struck up a conversation with the only other person there, it turned out that the kind, white-haired woman was his second cousin, a chance encounter that lifted his troubled spirits. As an only son of an only son, my father was, I realised late in life, frequently alone – one reason, I assume, that he had maintained friendships since childhood.

When I picture my father, he is always in fast motion: striding, driving, singing, smoking and drinking. There was an intensity to him even when he was reading, as his entire body focused on the pages of a book. After a childhood living between Naples, Luxor and Fontainebleau, he continued to travel, including a road trip to India in the 1960s, as part of a University of Cambridge acting company. In the early 1980s he spent a British summer in Australia and late in his teaching career he managed to find stints of teaching most years, in Barbados or Manhattan. He would return full of stories, always about the people he met, and often with generous gifts. After one such trip to New York, he returned with a document for me signed by the abolitionist and writer Frederick Douglass, which he had bought, on a whim, in a bookshop.

In the last few years before he moved into his care home, travel became a source of great anxiety for my father, who fretted about train tickets, passports and arriving on time. Train rides to Edinburgh, which were once spent reading and chatting, were now filled with disquiet as my father checked his pockets for tickets every few minutes, his face contorted in perturbation. During his last few years of good health, he took great pleasure in pootling down the Shropshire Union Canal in a small river cruiser that he and my mother had bought, until that last vestige of independence, along with his driving licence, was taken away. When he moved to the care home, my father wandered the corridors, and in and out of the other residents' rooms. He would stay awake all night, rarely sitting down, before finally collapsing, as though jet-lagged, wherever exhaustion found him, which was rarely his own room, the vestiges of his life misplaced or displaced, like his place in our world.

~~~~~

In Baldwin's writing, journeys, like stories, can be difficult to embark upon and perilous to finish. It is striking how travelling in his fiction and non-fiction is rarely romanticised. In *Giovanni's Room*, the eponymous protagonist is an economic migrant, who left his southern Italian village to make a living in Paris, while David, a white middle-class American, has moved to the City of Light to 'find himself'. David grew up in Brooklyn, San Francisco, Seattle and New York, and Paris gives him the illusion of freedom – 'with no-one to watch, no penalties attached'. But after falling in love with Giovanni, David feels trapped in his lover's tiny room, and imprisoned in his belief that he must be heterosexual. And while David had fled the United States to find himself, the novel begins and ends with him alone, with just enough self-awareness to make his situation unbearable: 'There is something fantastic in the spectacle I now present to myself of having run so far, so hard, across the ocean even, only to find myself brought up short once more before the bulldog in my own backyard'.[50]

In Baldwin's last novel, *Just Above My Head*, the protagonist, Arthur Montana, a Harlemite who is known as 'The Emperor of Soul', dies alone in a London pub, while another character, Julia, bears a striking resemblance to her creator. Like Baldwin, Julia was a child preacher who suffered at the hands of an abusive father, whose line about leaving the church – 'Sometimes, now that I'm out of the pulpit, I feel more *in* the pulpit than I did when I was preaching' – could have been lifted from an interview with the author.[51] Looking for redemption, and to find her place in the world, Julia lives in the West African city of Abidjan for two years. In Africa she meets a '*really* black' man who is old enough to be her father, the only male who 'understood something' about her, but her journey to Africa is beset by linguistic and cultural obstacles.[52] 'A black girl in Africa', Julia concludes, 'who wasn't *born* in Africa ... is a very strange creature for herself, and for everyone who meets her'.[53]

A snapshot of Baldwin's relationship to African culture, and of his frenetic travelling schedule, is captured in letters to his then agent, Robert P. Mills, that were published in *Harper's Magazine* in May 1963. In 1961, Baldwin left Paris for Israel, then went on to Istanbul and then Switzerland before travelling to West Africa in 1962, where he had been assigned to write a piece for the *New Yorker*. Baldwin's letters, very few of which have been published, demonstrate his preter-natural talent as a writer. They are philosophical, warm and thought-provoking, giving readers an unprecedented insight into his unedited and intimate prose.

A visit to Jerusalem led Baldwin to reflect on his place in the world and to ponder his forthcoming trip to Sierra Leone, Guinea, Liberia and the Ivory Coast. 'My bones know, somehow, something of what waits for me in Africa', Baldwin wrote to his agent. 'That is one of the reasons I have dawdled so long – I'm afraid ... it would be nice to be able to dream about Africa, but once I have been there, I will not be able to dream anymore'.[54] As he reflected on this upcoming trip, Baldwin's letters reveal his thoughts on Black American con-nections to the continent.[55]

Baldwin's much anticipated trip to West Africa was beset with logistical challenges, including problems with visas, the kind of detail at which the writer did not excel. And rather than furnishing him with new material for the *New Yorker*, or perhaps for a short story or two, Baldwin's typewriter resisted, just as it did not produce substantial writing about his prolonged visits to Turkey during the 1960s. Travelling, for Baldwin, rather enabled him to think more keenly about his place in the world, about his American identity and about his status as an expatriate writer: 'one thing which this strange and lonely journey has made me feel even more strongly', Baldwin wrote from Turkey, 'is that it's much better for me to try and stay out of the US as much as possible'.[56] But if the United States was too menacing, a country in which he found it hard to focus and write, then France, by then his adopted country for fifteen years, was not yet a place he called home. Torn between the need to live outside of the United States and guilt at not witnessing the daily struggle for civil rights – but acknowledging that he could only write with critical and emotional distance – travel, rather than a fixed notion of home and place, seemed to drive his writing. 'I think that I must really reconcile myself to being a transatlantic commuter', he wrote, 'and turn to my advantage, and not impossibly the advantage of others, the fact that I am a stranger everywhere'.[57] Baldwin's references to being a stranger seem closely connected to what it means to be strange or queer, raising pressing questions about his self-imposed exile. 'Abroad I became freer', he explained in an interview, a comment that cuts across relationships to writing.[58] Did he struggle to focus and write in the United States, or did he find it difficult to live and love in the country of his birth? Or was it both? Did he need critical distance from his homeland, as he sometimes intuited, or did living abroad allow him an erotic and emotional connection to everyday life?

Over the last two decades, scholars and writers have documented Baldwin's sojourns in, and relationship to, France and Turkey, but there is little on his complicated relationship to the United Kingdom and to British culture. Long before he had visited the British capital, the teenage Baldwin wrote a short story, 'Incident in London', for *Magpie*, his high-school magazine. Baldwin frequently alluded to Dickens as an inspiration, but there is not much in this brief short story that gives it a sense of place. 'Incident in London', which is not much longer than most liner notes for an album, is about an unnamed veteran who is drawn to a small chapel, believing it to be a refuge 'from strife and from fear'.[59] As he enters the chapel, however, 'a roar of fury filled the universe' and 'slowly the chapel crumbled to the white, still earth'. The chapel is destroyed 'and the snow was no longer pure, but filthy, and the man was dead'.

'Incident in London', written when Baldwin was around seventeen – the age that he left the church – bears the hallmarks of the author's considerable, and understandable, teenaged angst. This was around the time that he was preparing to leave his role as an evangelical child preacher, when he was struggling to come to terms with his sexuality, and when he was gearing up to leave home. When Baldwin describes the obliteration of a chapel, and the church's failure to give refuge and succour to the damaged veteran, it is hard not to read the story in the light of his profound disillusionment with the church. The story also bears the scars of juvenilia, including one livid line in which 'the stars winked and trembled in the heavens', but the tone and mood are accomplished, and there are one or two portentous trademark lines.[60] The description of the snow as 'no longer pure, but filthy' anticipates 'Stranger in the Village' (published in 1953), where is he surrounded by ice-capped mountains, which concludes with the sentence 'This world is white no longer, and it will never be white again'.[61] Pre-empting the near future when African countries would gain independence, and when much of US white society was concerned about racial mixing in the wake of the desegregation of schools in 1954, Baldwin's critique of white purity is prescient and timely. In 1952, the year before Baldwin published *Go Tell It on the Mountain*, Ralph Ellison's *Invisible Man* exposed the fictions of white identity. The nameless narrator works for Liberty Paints and discovers that the 'Optic White' emulsion, which is sold with the slogan 'It's the Right White', achieves its seeming brilliant white purity by mixing in black paint.

Baldwin's decision to call his story 'Incident in London' may well have been a way to distance himself from the subject matter. It's a story, after all, about a veteran who seeks refuge in the church, only to be destroyed with it, which would have displeased his stepfather. Between the early 1950s and the mid-1980s, Baldwin visited London on numerous occasions, as well as making trips to Edinburgh and to Hull (he was awarded an honorary doctorate by the University of Hull in 1976). These trips included visits to the United Kingdom in 1949 and 1955 when he was respectively trying to establish magazine contacts and trying to drum up interest in his first play, *The Amen Corner* (1955).

Baldwin's relationship to the United Kingdom has intrigued me for years. When I started researching Baldwin in the late 1990s, during a time when the writer was decidedly unfashionable, even *passé*, I wrote to James Campbell, a London-based writer whose biography of Baldwin I had read many times. I spent a weekend in the attic room of Campbell's flat, poring over copies of letters written by Baldwin, an experience that spurred me on to find out as much about the writer as I could.

A decade or so later I met George Solomos, also known as Themistocles Hoetis, a close friend of Baldwin in the late 1940s and a native of Detroit. Along with Asa Benveniste, a New York-born poet and publisher, he founded *Zero* in 1949, the first English-language literary magazine to be published in France after the Second World War. The first issue included poetry by John Goodwin and William Carlos Williams, along with a short story by Christopher Isherwood.

Midway through that issue, Richard Wright's story 'The Man Who Killed a Shadow' sits before Baldwin's 'Everybody's Protest Novel', an essay that announced him as a serious writer on both sides of the Atlantic and a piece in which he attacked Wright, his former mentor.

When I met Solomos in the early 2000s, he was living in south-east London. His health was poor but his creative antennae were still quivering. As soon as I entered his flat, he took my photograph, correctly guessed my star sign and told me that I reminded him of Benveniste, who strangely enough is buried not far from where I live in West Yorkshire, in the same graveyard as the poet Sylvia Plath. But while the latter's grave is festooned with pens and the occasional sheaf of poems, Benveniste's is, well, as quiet as the grave. It's worth a visit, if only to read the inscription: 'Foolish enough to have been a poet'.

On my first visit to Solomos's flat, he offered me something 'very mild' to smoke at eleven o'clock in the morning, which I accepted, then regretted. He regaled me with stories about his wife, Gidske Anderson, a writer and journalist who later chaired the Norwegian Nobel Committee. Solomos and Baldwin were both homosexual, but both were keen to marry Anderson. In the late 1940s, Baldwin had referred to her as 'the Norwegian who saved my life', and he would later refer to her as his fiancée.[62] Solomos told me that his friendship with Baldwin was never quite the same after his marriage to Anderson.

While there are several detailed accounts of the writer in Turkey and France, Baldwin's intriguing relationship to Britain remains uncharted. It can be said, though, that the writer regarded Britain with unwavering ambivalence. His association with the country started well. Baldwin, who had been unable to find a publisher in the United States for

Giovanni's Room, secured a deal with the London publisher Michael Joseph, which later became an imprint of Penguin Books. He loved Britain, he told an *Observer* journalist in 1967, 'because Dickens lived here', a comment he revised five years later.[63] 'I may have been romantic about London – because of Charles Dickens', Baldwin explained, 'but that romance lasted for exactly as long as it took me to carry my bags out of Victoria Station'.[64] Asked by the sociologist Paul Gilroy (many years later) why he had settled in Paris rather than in London, Baldwin replied:

> It would have seemed logical for both Richard [Wright] and myself to have settled in the city of Charles Dickens, but I've never got on with the English in general. People who believe that an elderly British matron is Empress of the Indies and Queen of all Africa are dangerously removed from reality.[65]

In his comments about Britain, Baldwin frequently invokes his love of Dickens – and in particular *A Tale of Two Cities*, a historical novel set between London and Paris during the French Revolution. But over the years he frequently qualified his admiration for the Victorian writer by reminding his interviewers that Britain's conscience was as filthy as the snow in 'Incident in London' when it came to participation in the trade of enslaved African people and the empire. In February 1965, when Baldwin was in London following his debate with Buckley, a *Daily Mail* reporter quizzed him on his reaction to the assassination of Malcolm X. Baldwin made it clear that he 'could never forget that London was the capital of the slavers', reminding his interviewer of Britain's role in the Caribbean slave trade, as well as the history of colonialism in the continent of Africa.[66]

Three years later, Baldwin recalled renting a house in Chelsea, London, during which time he gave his talk at the

West Indian Students' Centre. Reflecting on his trip to the British capital, Baldwin recalled that 'London was reacting to its accelerating racial problem and compounding the disaster by denying it had one'.[67] Over the next two decades, Baldwin was a regular visitor to Britain, and to London in particular. In 1971, he gave a speech at Central Hall in Westminster in support of three young African American men – George Jackson, John Clutchette and Fleeta Drumgo – known, after the California prison in which they were held, as the Soledad Brothers. The men were accused of killing a white prison officer at San Quentin Prison in 1970, a penitentiary north of San Francisco that was the setting for Johnny Cash's famous live recording the year before. In late 1970, Baldwin had spoken in defence of the Soledad Brothers in Paris, along with the French writer Jean Genet. At his brief speech in London, Baldwin invoked the names of Richard Nixon and Enoch Powell, adding 'I don't want to speak about your country, I'm a guest here!', either because he was exercising uncharacteristic restraint or because he was on much less familiar political terrain when it came to British politics.

Within a few months of his speech in Westminster, Baldwin was back in the British capital to record a television show with the younger Black American poet Nikki Giovanni; their conversation was later transcribed and published as *A Dialogue* (1973). The conversation, which is fractious in places, exposed the ways that the older writer was giving ground to poets such as Giovanni who found their voice during the revolutionary era of the late 1960s. During the 1970s Baldwin was no longer deemed to be a vital force in American letters, but in the following decade he started to achieve a renaissance of sorts. He wrote the introduction to a new edition of *Notes of a Native Son*, a collection of essays that remained fresh thirty years after its first publication.

PBS broadcast an adaptation of *Go Tell It on the Mountain* in 1985, a year which also marked the publication of his essay *The Evidence of Things Not Seen*, as well as *The Price of the Ticket*, a collection of his non-fiction.

Between January and March 1987, his debut play, *The Amen Corner*, first staged at Howard University in 1955, but not published in its entirety until 1968, enjoyed a successful run at the Tricycle Theatre – now the Kiln Theatre – in Kilburn, London. And when it transferred to London's Lyric Theatre in Shaftesbury Avenue, *The Amen Corner* became the first all-Black production to transfer from the Fringe to the West End.

At the invitation of the director, Anton Phillips, Baldwin met with the cast during the show's final rehearsals. In an interview at the time with the Welsh broadcaster Mavis Nicholson, Baldwin's visceral charisma almost masks his frail body, by then consumed with cancer of the oesophagus, which would hasten his death later that year. In a wide-ranging discussion of the play and its enduring themes, Baldwin returned to a discussion of his stepfather. In *The Amen Corner*, however, it is Sister Margaret, a pious and embittered preacher, who most closely resembles David Baldwin, while Luke, her estranged husband, a jazz musician, teaches her what it means to live and to love. As Baldwin told Nicholson, many people hide behind faith 'to avoid confronting love. And love involves the terrors of life and that involves the terrors of death'.[68]

The Amen Corner explores the manner in which religion can get in the way of relationships – how pious people can be immune to change and to the experiences of those around them. It is also a play about making mistakes. At the end of the play, Margaret realises that she has preached about love but has not experienced it, and that her seemingly feckless and wayward jazz-musician husband has much to teach her about the price of the ticket. In the introduction to the published script of the play, Baldwin recalls that the first sentence he wrote of it, which appears in the third act, is 'It's an awful thing to think about, the way love never dies!' – a line which I think about each time I visit my father as I am wracked with guilt for not visiting him often. Baldwin's sentiment – that love never dies – gives me succour as each encounter with my father diminishes the version of him that I treasure, as well as fuelling fear that he is what I will become.[69] Or, as Baldwin puts it in relation to his father, 'when I began to think about what had happened to him, I began to see why he was so terrified of what was surely going to happen to me'.[70]

Chapter 4

Mistakes, we'd made a few,
too many to mention

We must speak of failure, abomination, and death, not to drive our readers to despair, but on the contrary, to try to save them from despair.

Simone de Beauvoir, 'What Can Literature Do?' (1965)

Success is too often confused with financial gain. I have known many successful people with no money and there are plenty of millionaires who have failed to make a mark where it counts.

Richard Field, in conversation with the
author (around ten years ago)

You know you have made it when your face appears on a prayer candle. Entrepreneurs are selling a 'James Baldwin Secular Saint Candle', enabling consumers to 'Show ... devotion to James Baldwin, patron saint of poets, uncles and exiles'. Baldwin merchandise ranges from T-shirts emblazoned with 'Baby, they gonna burn your house down' to at least one book of quotations by the author. In fact, it's possible to furnish a house with Baldwin posters, coasters, candles, stickers and duvet covers. And if your coffee table is looking bare, then you can seek guidance from the *Daily Beast*, where a new edition of *Nothing Personal*, Baldwin's photo-text collaboration from the 1960s, was listed in 2017 as one of the 'Best coffee table books'.

One of the most ubiquitous Baldwin quotations, which floats around social media but can also be found stitched on chiastic cushions, is 'Not everything that is faced can be changed; but nothing can be changed until it is faced', a line, when decontextualised, which makes the writer sound like an aspiring life coach. The quotation is taken from 'As Much Truth As One Can Bear', a piece that first appeared in the *New York Times Book Review* in 1962. It was omitted from his *Collected Essays* but republished in a volume of his hitherto uncollected writings, *The Cross of Redemption*. The article, written as Baldwin was starting to gain notoriety as an author, is a thought-provoking meditation on the state of American literature. Baldwin observes how white canonical authors, among them Ernest Hemingway, F. Scott Fitzgerald and William Faulkner, 'have acquired such weight and become so sacrosanct that they have been used as touchstones to reveal the understandable, but lamentable, inadequacy of the younger literary artists'.[1]

Sixty years on from the publication of 'As Much Truth As One Can Bear', and as the centennial of his birth arrives, the coffee tables have turned. When Baldwin wrote that 'it seems to me, the adulation so cruelly proffered our elders has nothing to do with their achievement', he was taking aim at canonical writers, a mantle that he is now fast acquiring. The essay titles 'Nobody Knows My Name' and 'No Name in the Street', which once reflected the author's uncertain place in the world, began to seem ironic from the early 1960s, reflected by the title of Marvin Elkoff's article on Baldwin in the August 1964 title of *Esquire*, 'Everybody Knows His

Name'. Now, as many commentators have noted, Baldwin 'is everywhere'.

In an interview with *Esquire*, conducted days after he returned from Martin Luther King Jr.'s funeral on 9 April 1968 (but published some months later), Baldwin spoke about the spate of riots that tore through US cities, including Baltimore, Boston, Cleveland and Washington, DC. 'I don't believe what I read in the newspapers', Baldwin told his interviewer, adding, 'I object to the term "looters" because I wonder who is looting whom, baby'.[2]

Baldwin was a master of oratory and rhetoric. One of his most effective techniques was to reflect questions and assumptions back to his interviewer or reader. 'It's not the Negro problem', he explained to an audience, 'it's the white problem. I'm only black because you *think* you're white'.[3] 'I wonder who is looting whom' follows this pattern in Baldwin's thinking by tilting the interviewer and reader away from their fixed position. African Americans, Baldwin's response intuits, have been robbed of selfhood and denied civil rights, acts of ontological vandalism and political theft that make the looting of a few shops seem insignificant.

Baldwin's writing about the 1960s remains depressingly relevant today. In an essay called 'The White Man's Guilt', which was published six months after the assassination of Malcolm X in 1965, Baldwin implored white Americans to take responsibility for the narrative of American history. Published as Alabama state troopers had beaten protesters in Selma and as riots tore through Watts, a large neighbourhood in southern Los Angeles, Baldwin reminded his readers that the narrative of America's history of racial oppression could be – and must be – changed, a process that would cause 'great pain and terror', since it required the upheaval of history's 'tyrannical power'.[4]

During the resuscitation of Baldwin's career in the decades following his death, he is frequently described as a prophet. The title of a posthumous collection of Baldwin's writings, *The Cross of Redemption*, is in keeping with this description. A recent book is called *The Gospel According to James Baldwin: What America's Great Prophet Can Teach Us about Life, Love, and Identity* and there are scores of articles and radio programmes with titles such as 'Return of the Prophet: Baldwin in the Twenty-First Century'. Baldwin was a singularly perceptive cultural and political commentator, but to describe him as 'prophetic' takes away the skills that he honed as a writer and observer, just as Billie Holiday is often described as a naturally gifted singer, with no acknowledgement of her skill as a musician. Prophets are born with their insight, or it is bestowed upon them, while writers, like other artists, graft to hone their craft.

Describing Baldwin as a prophet also sanitises the author and his work; it not only airbrushes out his flaws and contradictions, but it also aligns the writer with a notion of purity that his writing fiercely contests. In one of his earliest essays, 'Everybody's Protest Novel', Baldwin critiques Harriet Beecher Stowe's hugely successful novel *Uncle Tom's Cabin*, drawing attention to the ways that the titular character is so pious that he 'has been robbed of his humanity and divested of his sex'.[5] One of Baldwin's earliest published stories is called 'The Death of the Prophet'; in it, the teenaged protagonist abandons the faith that is central to his puritanical father, a theme that cuts across much of his writing.

Go Tell It on the Mountain, which develops many of his short story's preoccupations, is characterised by a series of powerful recurring tensions, including a refusal to renounce, mortify or ignore the body. Throughout the novel, Baldwin explores how the distinctions between the broad and narrow

ways – the worldly and the saintly – and between the flesh and
the Word, sinner and saved, are not only damaging dichoto-
mies, but are fabrications which always threaten to break
down. And, indeed, much of Baldwin's work explores the
tensions between religion and sexuality. As John, the teenage
protagonist, cleans the church, his thoughts turn from the
abstractions of the Lord to the 'odour of dust and sweat' that
overwhelms his senses.[6] The act of worship, Baldwin reminds
us, requires the body as well as the spirit to participate: when
'praying or rejoicing', the bodies of the worshippers 'gave off
an acrid, steamy smell, a marriage of the odours of dripping
bodies and soaking, starched white linen', an earthy and
sensual odour that is reminiscent of the smells of dust, sweat
and gin found on Broadway, the temptation-soaked Badlands
outside of the church.[7] When the pastor's nephew, Elisha,
is 'saved', this sacred moment is marked not by his spiritual
rebirth but by the physicality of his trembling body, as 'his
thighs moved terribly against the cloth of his suit'.[8] When
he is later publicly reprimanded for 'walking disorderly' with
a teenage parishioner, Ella Mae, Baldwin describes how her
'white robes now seemed to be the merest, thinnest covering
for the nakedness of breasts and insistent thighs'.[9] During
the church service, Baldwin suggests that sexual energy and
desire are at times indistinguishable from religious ecstasy,
illustrated by his description of Elisha playing the piano: 'At
one moment, head thrown back, eyes closed, sweat standing
on his brow, he sat at the piano, singing and playing; and then
... he stiffened and trembled, and cried out, *Jesus, Jesus, oh
Lord Jesus!*'[10]

In Baldwin's second novel, his all-American protagonist,
David, refuses to admit his love for the eponymous Giovanni
because he insists on maintaining his purity, with the
corollary that love for another man is impure. It is only at the

end of the novel, when David has experienced both love and loss, that he understands his salvation is hidden in his flesh, a theme that anticipates Baldwin's final novel, *Just Above My Head* (1979), where Jimmy states that 'every inch' of his lover, Arthur, 'was sacred to me'.[11]

Throughout his writing, Baldwin celebrates the body, which is elevated rather than mortified. In his description of Jesus Christ, the son of God is portrayed as a rabble-rouser – a 'disreputable sun-baked Hebrew', rather than an otherworldly alabaster statue.[12] In his last published essay, 'To Crush the Serpent', which appeared in *Playboy* magazine in 1987, Baldwin critiqued the ways that the Reaganite 'Moral Majority' had increasingly become aligned with neoliberalism and conservatism. In a passage that would have outraged evangelical Christian readers, he argued that even holy men go the way their blood beats: 'Nowhere, in the brief and extraordinary passage of the man known as Jesus Christ, is it recorded that he ever upbraided his disciples concerning their carnality. These were rough, hard-working fishermen on the Sea of Galilee.'[13]

Fifteen years earlier, Baldwin went even further in a conversation with the poet Nikki Giovanni, when he complained that casting doubt on the dogma of the immaculate conception led to accusations of sacrilege. 'I think the legend itself is a blasphemy', Baldwin told the poet. 'What is wrong with a man and a woman sleeping together, making love to each other and having a baby like everybody else? Why does the son of God have to be born immaculately? Aren't we all the sons of God? That's the blasphemy.'[14]

In the spring of 2014, *New York Times* journalist Felicia Lee observed that James Baldwin's presence was fading from North American classrooms. Baldwin, it seemed, had been eclipsed by other African American voices.[15] After the shooting of Michael Brown in Ferguson, Missouri, later that year by a white police officer, however, Baldwin, who died in 1987, was claimed as the most frequently tweeted literary authority of the Black Lives Matter movement. Between 2014 and 2015, the most tweeted Baldwin quotation reflects on the role of white policemen, ending with the line 'Negroes want to be treated like [humans]'.[16] By August of 2018, which was the month of the writer's birthday, there were over 90,000 tweets referring to Baldwin.

From the late 1960s, Baldwin's career threatened to re-ignite, but in fact for the most part his reputation dwindled. Around the start of the century critics started to re-appraise his writing, and a decade later his life and work were back in the public imagination. Ta-Nehisi Coates's bestselling *Between the World and Me* (2015) drew heavily on Baldwin; in 2016, Raoul Peck's *I Am Not Your Negro* similarly brought Baldwin's life and work to new audiences, while Barry Jenkins's adaptation of Baldwin's 1974 novel *If Beale Street Could Talk* (2018) received positive reviews on both sides of the Atlantic. Most recently, Eddie Glaude Jr.'s work of non-fiction *Begin Again: James Baldwin's America and Its Urgent Lessons for Our Own* (2020) suggests how it is possible to make sense of, and learn from, the racial quagmire of President Trump's tenure through a reading of the writer's life and work.

Baldwin's renaissance as a hip, relevant writer coincided with the emergence, and then backlash against, woke culture and virtue-signalling. In 'A Letter on Justice and Open Debate', published in *Harper's Magazine*, which was signed by scores of writers – among them John Banville, Martin Amis and Salman Rushdie – the signatories testified to a growing culture of censure, rather than debate. 'Censoriousness is also spreading more widely in our culture', the letter proclaimed, 'an intolerance of opposing views, a vogue for public shaming and ostracism, and the tendency to dissolve complex policy issues in a blinding moral certainty'.[17]

During the recent culture wars, and as questions of free speech and cancel culture have rumbled on, Baldwin's name has frequently been invoked. In 2017, Teju Cole, a Nigerian-American writer and photographer – and an admirer of the writer's work – observed that Baldwin had become the 'go-to quote factory for those who are "woke" on social media'.[18] But as Thomas Chatterton Williams cautioned a few years later, 'people channeling Baldwin aren't really channeling Baldwin' but, rather, cherry-picking facets of his writing life to suit their own cultural and political agendas.[19] Williams, an astute commentator on Baldwin's life and work, has urged readers to be mindful of the ways that the writer's work has been co-opted into the culture wars. 'To be black and conscious in America is to be in a constant state of rage' is one of the most recycled quotations from Baldwin across social media, but it has a contested provenance. In *The White Album* (1979), Joan Didion claims that Eldridge Cleaver wrote the phrase down, who in turn was quoting the Black Panther leader Huey P. Newton, who had heard the line from Baldwin. The quotation – albeit in a slightly different form – was in fact uttered by Baldwin on a WBAI Radio show in New York on 10 January 1961, on a programme called *The Negro in American Culture*, which included contributions from Langston Hughes and Lorraine Hansberry. Early in the discussion, in response to a question about the polarity he experienced as an African American and a writer, Baldwin replied: 'to be a Negro in this country and to be relatively conscious is to be in a rage almost all the time', a line that is frequently quoted inaccurately, and without context. The factory, it seems, also produces counterfeits, or at least products with dubious provenance. As Baldwin cautions on the same radio programme – a warning which has lost none of its relevance – 'it's a great temptation to simplify the issues under the illusion that if you simplify them enough, people will recognise them; and this illusion is very dangerous because that isn't the way it works'.

In an article published a few years ago, Benin Bryant pondered the damaging effects of cancel culture on both sides of the Atlantic and on both sides of the political spectrum. To illustrate his point, Bryant looked back to the debate at Cambridge University in 1965, where Buckley's suave confidence was no match for Baldwin's rhetorical left hooks. During his speech, Buckley played down the importance of Baldwin's racial identity, claiming it was irrelevant to their debate. Bryant makes the point that Buckley's comments would not have escaped moderation during the 2020s, and that his claim that racial segregation was a temporary necessity would have caused him to be 'cancelled'. Or, to use the inelegant term for when individuals have been removed from public debate in recent years, it is likely that Buckley would have been 'de-platformed'. 'What is certain', Bryant concludes, 'is that the brilliance of Baldwin's debate performance was, in part, only evident due to the juxtaposition of his ideas against Buckley's'.[20]

Throughout his long career Baldwin inveighed against the dangers of blindly following ideologies, whether on the right or the left of the political spectrum. Truth, he cautioned, 'is not to be confused with ... devotion to a Cause ... Causes, as we know, are notoriously bloodthirsty'.[21] In his first major essay, Baldwin takes the protest novel to task in a language that carries strong echoes of virtue-signalling. He acknowledges the 'good intentions' of those protest novels that purport to expose the damaging effects of racism, but concludes that it does little to transform the reader, just as reading the *Guardian* or the *New York Times* does not necessarily make people become better citizens. 'Whatever unsettling questions are raised are evanescent, titillating', Baldwin writes, and he adds that 'finally we receive a very definite thrill of virtue from the fact that we are reading such a book at all'.[22]

In his interviews and essays Baldwin appeals for moral and intellectual complexity, qualities which he sees as sorely lacking in the culture of the United States of America, which he describes as 'a country devoted to the death of the paradox'.[23] Confronting what is challenging – especially when it seems irresolvable or hopeless – is crucial in Baldwin's schema, otherwise, as he bluntly puts it, 'we perish'. Baldwin goes as far as to say that it is 'only within this web of ambiguity, paradox, this hunger, danger, darkness, [that] can we find at once ourselves and the power that will free us from ourselves', a position that is echoed in the singer-songwriter Nick Cave's insistence on mercy.[24] Writing in his blog *The Red Hand Files*, the singer opines that 'Mercy ultimately acknowledges that we are all imperfect and in doing so allows us the oxygen to breathe – to feel protected within a society, through our mutual fallibility'. Art, Cave explains, can and should unsettle our most cherished positions: 'Creativity is an act of love that can knock up against our most foundational beliefs, and in doing so brings forth fresh ways of seeing the world'.[25]

One of the enduring images of Baldwin from the 1960s is of the author battling with white liberal interviewers on television shows during a distant era when writers drank, chain-smoked and debated. Baldwin's large eyes never seem to blink; he gesticulates with a cigarette in a manner that is suave but also menacing. His argument darts back and forth with lethal precision, its syntactical elegance belying a piercing uppercut. Baldwin speaks in paragraphs; his adversaries speak in sentences. And while the writer did not always get it right – at times expressing clumsy views on patriarchy and Jewish culture – debate was something that he saw as essential during his career as a writer and speaker.

During the 1960s, Baldwin had several high-profile arguments with fellow writers, including Norman Mailer, a dissentient being who could start a fight in a Buddhist temple. In J. Michael Lennon's biography *Norman Mailer: A Double Life*, there are allusions to more than twenty brawls, including an incident with Gore Vidal on the *Dick Cavett* show in 1971. When Vidal justifiably tore into an article that Mailer had written in the *New York Review of Books* about women's liberation, Mailer – who had stabbed his wife, Adele Morales, in 1960 – responded by headbutting Vidal in the green room of the television studio. Baldwin and Mailer did not come to physical blows, but their fast-and-firm friendship, forged in Paris during the mid-1950s, had cooled off by the following decade. Mailer's discussion of Baldwin in his collection of essays, *Advertisements for Myself* (1959), won't have done much to cement their friendship. 'Baldwin seems incapable of saying "fuck you" to the reader', Mailer claimed, adding that 'even his best sentences are sprayed with perfume', a cheap swipe at Baldwin's sexuality. *Giovanni's Room*, Mailer concludes, is 'brave' but 'bad', a comment that anticipates his post-mortem of *Another Country*, which he deemed to be 'abominably written'.[26]

Mailer's pugnacious dismissal concludes by urging Baldwin to 'smash the perfumed dome of his ego' if he is to

avoid remaining a 'minor'.[27] (When Mailer died, the *Guardian*
ran an obituary with the title 'Farewell to Norman Mailer, a
Sexist, Homophobic Reactionary', suggesting that it was he,
rather than Baldwin, who was more likely to be consigned to
the realm of minor writer.) Baldwin reflected on their friendship and its subsequent denouement in an article published
in *Esquire* magazine, the publication in which his friend-
turned-adversary became a household name. In 'The Black
Boy Looks at the White Boy', (1961), he claimed that Mailer
did not understand love and was obsessed with power. But it
was Mailer's refusal to give up 'that myth of the sexuality of
Negroes' which drove a wedge between the two writers.[28] In
an article for *Dissent* in 1957, a recently formed left-leaning
intellectual magazine, Mailer contributed an essay called
'The White Negro', which was written under a heady cocktail
of influences, including the absinthe of existentialism and
the hard liquor of the Beat Generation. Published the same
year as Jack Kerouac's second novel, *On the Road*, Mailer's
essay explores the role of the hipster as the United States
tilted towards Cold War conservatism.

Mailer's essay begins with an analysis of what the British
polymath Jeff Nuttall later called Bomb Culture, the palpable
and terrifying realisation that society could be obliterated
at the press of a button: 'Probably, we will never be able
to determine the psychic havoc of the concentration camps
and the atom bomb upon the unconscious mind of almost
everyone alive in these years'.[29] And in sharp contrast to
most Americans, who seemed oblivious to their fate, which
he called 'a slow death by conformity', the hipster, who
embraced death and who existed on the margins of society,
was receptive to 'the domain of experience'. In Mailer's logic,
hipsters are white men whose alienation from society is
modelled on the Black urban experience, since 'Hated from

outside and therefore hating himself, the Negro was forced into the position of exploring all those moral wildernesses of civilized life which the Square automatically condemns'.

Nearly a decade later, the African American writer Amiri Baraka, then known as LeRoi Jones, who began his career in Beat circles, argued that Black American culture was created in the hinterlands of mainstream America. Black Americans 'could not participate in the dominant tenor of the white man's culture', Jones explains, and 'it was this boundary, this no-man's-land' which became the source of creativity, and in particular music, a space hidden from white America.[30] Mailer's essay is also replete with references to African American jazz musicians, but his argument falls down as he first dips his toe in the brackish water of stereotypes and then plunges in headfirst. As he attempts to explain the sources of the Black urban experience, Mailer winks at received ideas before groping at typecasts of 'perversion, promiscuity, pimpery, drug addiction, rape, razor-slash', a litany of stock images about the African American experience that Baldwin sought to dismantle.

Mailer's despatches from what Baldwin called the 'sexual battlefield' did little to counter recalcitrant myths of Black sexual potency – in fact they did much to advance them. But Baldwin was also suspicious of Mailer's dalliance with the Beat Generation, and in particular the ways the Black American experience was romanticised by white iconoclasts during the early days of the Civil Rights Movement. A genera-tion previously, the poet Langston Hughes had described the Harlem Renaissance of the 1920s and early 1930s as a period 'when the Negro was in vogue'.[31] The audiences who flocked to 'Black' venues such as the Cotton Club in Harlem during the 1920s were in fact largely white in the early days; they forgot about Prohibition; they gulped down bootlegged bourbon as they listened to the predominantly Black maestros of the jazz world, among them Duke Ellington and Louis Armstrong.

During the mid-1950s, as the Civil Rights Movement got underway, African Americans were hardly in vogue, but several of the Beat Generation writers, including Allen Ginsberg and Jack Kerouac, wrote of their own disenchantment with middle America and their attraction to outsiders. Inmates of 'insane asylums', as they were called in the 1950s, including Carl Solomon, the dedicatee of Ginsberg's most famous poem, 'Howl', were the seers and vatics who were saner than the 'organization man', whose loyalty to corporations suppressed individual thought. Vagrants or 'bums', along with Black Americans and 'dope fiends', were extolled by the Beats for not conforming to the capitalist individualism of Cold War America. Ginsberg's 'Howl', composed during the early 1950s, begins 'I saw the best minds of my generation destroyed by madness, starving hysterical naked, / dragging themselves through the negro streets at dawn looking for an angry fix', lines which carry echoes of Mailer's fetishisation of urban Black American culture, which both writers associate with criminality and liminality.[32]

But it was the depictions of African American culture by Jack Kerouac, the reluctant 'King of the Beats', that most riled Baldwin. In 'The Black Boy Looks at the White Boy' Baldwin reflected on his relationship with Mailer, whom he associated with the current vogue of the Beat Generation. Baldwin's essay quotes a notorious passage from Kerouac's *On the Road* in which the narrator, Sal Paradise, 'walked with every muscle aching among the lights of 27th and Welton in the Denver colored section, wishing I were a Negro'.[33] Baldwin's response was unequivocal: he castigated Kerouac for a passage that was 'absolute nonsense' and 'offensive', adding, 'I would hate to be in Kerouac's shoes if he should ever be mad enough to read this aloud from the stage of Harlem's Apollo Theater'.[34] Baldwin's views on the Beats did not soften. In 'If Black English Isn't a Language, Then Tell Me, What Is?', published nearly twenty years later, he mused on the appropriation of Black vernacular by the Beats, a group composed of '*uptight*, middle-class white people, imitating poverty'; he points out that '*Beat to his socks*' 'was once the black's most total and despairing image of poverty' until it was commandeered – or 'appropriated' in today's parlance – by Kerouac, Ginsberg and others.[35] As early as 1959, in a review of Langston Hughes's *Selected Poems*, Baldwin noted how 'the white world takes over this [African American] vocabulary – without the faintest notion of what it really means'.[36]

In recent years, rumours circulated on social media that 'The White Negro' had been cancelled after a junior editor had objected to the title when a posthumous volume of Mailer's essays was planned for publication. The story was subsequently discredited; the decision not to publish the book had more to do with the declining sales of Mailer's work since the 1990s. The brief contretemps, in which commentators bemoaned the censure of Mailer's essay, nonetheless fed into debates about cultural appropriation and cancel culture, an arena in which nuance and cultural history are not always observed as doors are slammed shut. In sharp contrast, the philosopher Vilém Flusser, writing in the mid-1960s, explored the value of doubt, and said that it led to 'a polyvalent state of mind'. In moderate doses, he posited, doubt 'stimulates thought', leading thinkers towards the intricacies of the intellectual and moral patterns before them.[37]

Baldwin, who usually viewed culture through a nuanced lens, was keenly aware of Mailer's Jewishness, which he understood may have influenced his views on outsiders, just as Kerouac – who hailed from a French-Canadian family – learned to speak English only when he was six years old. And while Baldwin was deeply suspicious of Kerouac's references to jazz and the blues, both writers invoked music, rather than existentialism, to explore the condition of post-war US life. In musicians such as Charlie Parker, Kerouac and Baldwin recognised a distinctly American expression. In the preface to *Mexico City Blues* (1959), Kerouac wrote that he wanted 'to be considered a jazz poet blowing a long blues in an afternoon jam session', a description which anticipates Baldwin's claim three years later that 'I think I really help-lessly model myself on jazz musicians and try to write the way they sound'.[38] For Kerouac, Bop was 'the actual inner sound of a country', while for Baldwin his characters existed in 'another country', a place he suggests is unknown and un-knowable to the Beats, who plundered Black culture without understanding what he called 'the price of the ticket'.[39]

Some of Baldwin's most barbed comments on fellow writers are aimed at the Beat Generation, and at Kerouac in particular, whose confessional mode of writing he found woefully adolescent. 'It is masturbation. It is not writing', Baldwin told an interviewer in the early 1960s. 'I hate to say that, but it is true. I mean he's talented. So is everybody at the age of 5.'[40] Ouch. In his withering comments about Kerouac and his coterie, however, Baldwin omits to mention the contribution of several Black American authors to the Beat Generation. He does not mention Bob Kaufman's jazz-inflected poetry or Ted Joans's surrealist poetry and paintings, nor does he discuss the role of LeRoi Jones, who was an early and influential poet, editor and publisher of the Beat Generation, Black Mountain Poets and the New York School. And while Baldwin singles out Kerouac for his juvenile attempts at incorporating music into his work, jazz poetry has a longer and more entangled history, beginning with Langston Hughes's collection *The Weary Blues* (1926). A generation later, poets began reciting their verse to the accompaniment of jazz, but Kerouac was not the only cat in town. By 1958, the poet Kenneth Rexroth, who read jazz poetry in San Francisco's Cellar nightclub with the poet and publisher Lawrence Ferlinghetti, warned that it was becoming 'a fad'.[41] And while the male writers garnered more attention, the determinedly lower-case ruth weiss, a German-Austrian artist, was a pioneer of jazz poetry during the 1950s.

Baldwin's position on other cultural debates was not always easy to predict. During the complex shifting of the cultural landscape of the 1960s, he navigated his own course. By the start of that decade he was becoming a major writer. He had recently flown to Stockholm to interview the director Ingmar Bergman, followed by a trip to the South shadowing Martin Luther King Jr. With a salary of some $20,000 in 1961 – worth roughly ten times that amount in today's money – Baldwin had begun to obtain the success that he had craved. Never careful with his finances, Baldwin's love of whisky and late-night parties, as well as a growing entourage, left the writer with little money and no productive space in which to write. 'I am what you'd call a drinking man', Baldwin told a reporter from *Ebony* magazine in 1961.[42] Help came in the form of a fellow novelist, William Styron, who invited Baldwin to bring his typewriter with him to Connecticut. And while the writers' backgrounds were markedly different – one the grandchild of an enslaved person, the other the grandson of an enslaver – the months spent at Styron's guesthouse were remarkably productive for both authors. As one of Baldwin's biographers recounts, 'Meeting for lunch and dinner, Styron and Baldwin would discuss their work. Baldwin read aloud from *Another Country*, and Styron from *The Confessions of Nat Turner*.'[43]

The comfortable and collegial environment that helped to produce both novels contrasts sharply with their reception. *Another Country* was denounced in the *New Leader*, the magazine in which Baldwin had cut his teeth as a book reviewer, as 'degrading ... pornography'.[44] Styron's novel, published in 1967, was one of the most controversial books in decades. In a lengthy article for *Harper's Magazine* in 1965, Styron explained how Nat Turner, the leader of an insurrection of the enslaved in 1831, who had become 'erased from memory', had 'obsessed' his imagination.[45] In his introduction to the novel Styron insisted that he had 'rarely departed from the known facts about Nat Turner', defining his novel as less a 'historical novel in conventional terms than a meditation on history'.[46]

The Confessions of Nat Turner was initially lauded by critics. It won the Pulitzer Prize and became a *New York Times* bestseller – a paper which praised Styron as 'an expert in the Negro condition'.[47] But by the following year the novel was being denounced by many African American intellectuals as the Black Arts and Black Power Movements gained traction, arenas in which racial pride and self-determination became prominent. A volume of essays, *William Styron's Nat Turner: Ten Black Writers Respond*, argued that Styron's portrayal of the insurrection, far from being 'a meditation on history', deliberately distorted 'the true character of Nat Turner'.[48] Styron's Turner, one of the contributors argued, 'is not only the antithesis of Nat Turner; he is the antithesis of blackness ... a neurasthenic, Hamlet-like white intellectual in black face'.[49] Whereas much of the criticism challenged the ability and right of 'a white southern gentleman to tune in on the impulses, beliefs, emotions, and thought-patterns of a black slave', Baldwin stood apart from the majority of leading Black intellectuals.[50] Side-stepping the question of whether he should be allowed to write the novel, Baldwin spoke admiringly of how Styron 'had to put himself in the skin of Nat Turner' in order to 'deal with something that was tormenting him and frightening him'.[51] Over a decade later, Baldwin's position had not changed. 'My position was, and is (a) I am not about to tell another writer how and what to write.... And (b), if you don't like Styron's Nat Turner, write yours', a position echoed by Salman Rushdie.[52] In a recent interview, the author of *The Satanic Verses* stated: 'If we're in a world where only women can write about women and only people from India can write about people from India and only straight people can write about straight people ... then that's the death of the art'.[53]

On one level, Baldwin's support of Styron comes as little surprise. Aside from their friendship, Baldwin's choice of a white narrator in *Giovanni's Room* illustrated his conviction that an author could 'put himself in the skin' of a character, whether Black or white. Baldwin stated both that 'the words "white" and "black" don't mean anything' and that 'Color, for anyone who uses it, or is used by it, is a most complex, calculated and dangerous phenomenon'.[54]

In the early 1990s, Styron reflected that he had 'unwittingly created one of the first politically incorrect texts of our time'.[55] When I saw Styron give a lecture at the start of the millennium at Princeton University, the novel was not mentioned at all, not even by Toni Morrison, who introduced her fellow writer. During the Q&A I was too nervous to ask a question in the cavernous auditorium, and so I waited in vain for somebody to raise the controversy of his novel, which had caused protests at the prestigious university in the late 1960s. Styron, who was frail, and who struggled to read his talk without his glasses, seemed relieved to answer safe and somewhat banal questions, including 'Mr Styron, what are you working on now?'

The reception of *Giovanni's Room* and *The Confessions of Nat Turner* are reminders of the clinging assumptions, as Henry Louis Gates Jr. put it, that novels 'transparently convey the authentic, unmediated experience of the authors' social identities'.[56] Louis Simpson concluded that 'I am not sure it is possible for a Negro to write well without making us aware he is a Negro' and Irving Howe insisted that no white person could have written Ralph Ellison's *Invisible Man*, but other critics remain less certain.[57] Colin MacInnes, an astute reader of Baldwin, and whose novel *Absolute Beginners* (1959) was an early chronicle of multicultural London, wrote that *Giovanni's Room* is written 'so successfully that anyone who did not know what race he [is] ... could never guess ... that he was other than white himself'.[58] The writer W. J. Weatherby recalled his confusion at meeting Baldwin after reading *Giovanni's Room*: 'it never occurred to me that the author might be black', since there were no Black characters in the novel.[59]

Weatherby's assumption was by no means unique. When Dan McCall published *The Man Says Yes* in 1969, a novel about a young Black teacher, many critics assumed the author to be African American. The reviewer in the *Amsterdam News*, New York's oldest Black newspaper, referred to the author throughout as 'brother McCall' without realising that the author was white. Danny Santiago's *Famous All Over Town* (1983), set in a Los Angeles barrio, was praised by Latinx critics for its vibrancy and authenticity. The author in fact turned out to be Daniel James, a septuagenarian Yale-educated WASP.[60] A novel about a young Black man passing as white, *I Spit on Your Graves*, published in France shortly after the end of the Second World War, was reputedly written by Vernon Sullivan, a light-skinned African American author. Critics who had praised Sullivan's novel, comparing it to Richard Wright's *Native Son*, were less forthcoming when it transpired that Sullivan did not exist: he was merely the nom de plume of a white French writer, Boris Vian. The list could go on.

Perhaps what these novels all have in common is the difficulty in measuring cultural authenticity, to which Baldwin was keenly attuned. If, as Don L. Lee (Haki R. Madhubuti) asserted, 'a true test for a black poem is whether you can tell the author's color', then works such as *Giovanni's Room*, which sit uneasily in African American literature courses, continue to challenge such claims.[61] Nowhere is this more acutely illustrated that in the claim made by the jazz trumpeter Roy Eldridge to the critic Leonard Feather that he could distinguish white musicians from Black. As Mr Feather slid the needle into the grooves of recently released records – whose titles were concealed from the trumpeter – Eldridge began to segregate the Black musicians from the white. More than half the time, Eldridge got it wrong.[62]

Baldwin was fond of saying that 'an artist has always been a disturber of the peace', a role which does not sit easily with unchecked adulation, just as my father, whose generosity and capacity to listen, was counterbalanced with streaks of anger bordering on cruelty when his demand for truth and integrity was fuelled by alcohol.[63] As I reflect on Baldwin and my father, I am much more concerned with their contradictions and mistakes than in blemish-free accounts of each man.

In an interview published in *The Atlantic*, Megan Rapinoe reflected on her football career and on accusations that she does not 'love America' because she and some teammates chose not to sing the national anthem before matches. 'But we do love America', Rapinoe explained. 'It's just more in a James Baldwin kind of way, not in a bald-eagle-on-your-shoulder kind of way'.[64] Rapinoe's comment suggests she is familiar with Baldwin's views on patriotism, which he outlined in his short essay 'Autobiographical Notes'. 'I love America more than other country in the world', Baldwin explains, and 'exactly for this reason, I insist on the right to criticize her perpetually', a theme on which he riffed.[65] 'To be an American writer today', he wrote at the start of 1962 in 'As Much Truth As One Can Bear', 'means mounting an unending attack on all that Americans believe themselves to hold sacred'.[66]

Baldwin's insistence on the need for critical thinking – especially when the subject is sacrosanct – has helped me to reflect on my father. When I visit him in the care home, I am struck by his vulnerability, but his vacant stare also reminds me of the expression on his face when wine, followed by whisky, locked his eyes into an unblinking glassy gaze. During the late 1980s, my older sister and I grew adept at gauging the stages of our father's transformation. First came the stare, then the swaying, followed by accusations that circled around themselves, but which often ended in recrimination. When we tried to reason with him, or to make sense of his meandering points, he would rock back on his feet and mutter 'Hmmm', as though everyone else in the world were against him or were speaking untruths. During the first few bottles of wine, my father was funny and engaged. But when he turned – an unpoetic volta – his endearing qualities as a sensitive and engaged listener, along with his sense of humour, were suffocated by a menacing anger. In a state of seething inebriation, he believed that he was the defender of truth and integrity even as he lost track of his original point. In his dark mood, no one was safe from his attacks, which sprang not from cruelty or nastiness but from a fog of alcohol that shrouded the logic of his attack from those closest to him. At a certain stage of the evening, it became clear that he was waiting to pounce on anyone around him; a casual conversation became a battle to right wrongs only he knew about and which would be forgotten by the next morning.

He was deeply suspicious of couples who never argued, a point he made by driving my mother to such anger and frustration that, for a while, the sound of crockery hitting the walls was not unusual. I would seek refuge in my older sister's room as my mother implored my father to cut down on drinking and smoking, and he would storm out into the night and into their battered car in search of solitude and more alcohol. When he was arrested for drink driving he was more than three times over the legal limit, but the police officer remarked that he seemed sober until the breathalyser betrayed him. I recall recording him when he was drunk in the late 1980s as he seemed to have no awareness that he was making no sense, which now feels like a tragic foreshadowing of his current condition. He did not seem to notice as I placed the tape recorder in front of him, but I didn't have the courage to play it back to him the following day, not because he was unkind when sober but because I didn't want to humiliate him by introducing him to his demons, to which he seemed oblivious. Late on the night of his sixtieth birthday, he seemed deeply unhappy, uncharacteristically disappointed with the gifts his family had given him. Towards the end of the evening the alcohol took him over and he was in a dangerous mood. In the early hours of the morning he staggered into the doorway of each of his children's bedrooms, swaying and muttering barely audible accusations.

My father became locked into obsessions, or 'crazes' as we referred to them at home. He cultivated his future diabetes by devouring large quantities of Lion bars, Dime bars and Liquorice Allsorts. He watched his favourite film, *The Magnificent Seven*, six times in a week when it hit the cinema in 1961, and he would listen to the same album, or even song, over and over for hours at a time at our family home. He bought a recording of Ennio Morricone's soundtrack to the 1986 film *The Mission*, starring Robert De Niro and Jeremy Irons, which he listened to every evening for months at full volume with a bottle or two for company. (We cursed the friend who introduced him to Dire Straits.) He rarely cooked but when he discovered a recipe – spaghetti with a jar of clams or mussels drowning in wine – he would cook the dish so often that none of us could ever eat it again. The crazes extended to his intense friendships with men and women, which consumed his social life. There was a suspicion at home, not always unfounded, that these mutual infatuations crossed the boundaries of friendship and into another realm. I remember rooting through his chest of drawers in my early teens, just as I am rummaging through his life now. I found a leaflet about the local Alcoholics Anonymous programme, as well as a copy of the *Kama Sutra*, which was inscribed in my father's inimitable handwriting: 'To whomever finds this book, may they derive from it as much pleasure as it has given me'. My father embarrassed me during my youth, but I was always happy to be in his company. He wore bright trousers and talked to strangers wherever he went. He was at times aggressively sociable; someone who not only thrived but depended on interaction with strangers to affirm his place in the world, like a troubled Labrador. On one occasion he approached a busker, who was scratching a tired-looking violin, and asked him if he would stop playing for ten minutes if he paid him ten pounds. He took me camping most summers in the Brecon Beacons and we walked and talked all day, interrupted by long pub lunches during which my father struck up conversations with bar staff and fellow drinkers. I remember missing him terribly when he spent a summer in Australia and the delight at the boomerang and didgeridoo he brought back. He did not hold grudges and rarely disciplined me, placing faith in my ability to learn from my own mistakes. At times he showed me a bit too much trust. At the age of fifteen, as I started to learn Spanish, my parents bought me a train ticket to Barcelona. I spent three weeks travelling around Spain on my own, where I quickly spent my travellers' cheques on whisky and paella, sleeping under a car at Madrid train station, and contacting my family only once, via a postcard that arrived after I had returned.

My earliest memory of my father is when I was sitting on the floor of his study as he marked essays at his desk and I was mesmerised by the purplish wafts from his Marlboro cigarettes. When I grew older he told me to help myself to his tobacco, a ploy that worked for many years as I didn't see the point if there was no transgression. Alcohol was a different matter. Aged around four, I snuck along to a party that my parents held, where all the guests wore purple, a nod to the guru Bhagwan Shree Rajneesh, whose devotees wore the colours of the sun. I was fascinated by the picture of the guru my parents' guests wore around their necks, and I was unsure why adults left sweet-tasting drinks in their glasses, which I polished off, and then was found snoring under a table. On another occasion, aged around three, I glugged the contents of a decanter of sherry. A trip to the hospital was aborted after I threw up.

I don't think I fully understand my father, whose contradictions baffled me during my childhood, but which now I simply accept. As an only child with four children, he seemed unable or unwilling to navigate family life, illustrated by his solo walking-and-drinking holidays and his insistence that his offspring should enjoy visiting churches and pubs, rather than parks and playgrounds. He exuded a warmth that was palpable and magnetic, but he could also be withdrawn. As I tried to hold his hand at the funeral of his closest friend, he would not accept my offering, his eyes fixed ahead in solitary grief. When I picture him now, locked in his own half-thoughts, I think back to how he sought solitude among the family he helped to create. 'Funny how hard it is to be alone', he would quote from Philip Larkin, and '*All solitude is selfish*', lines that make me weep when I think of my father, solitary in his room.[67]

In late 1964, the critic Robert Brustein tore into *Nothing Personal* in a damning review. In sharp contrast to the *Daily Beast*'s praise of the book as a coffee-table must, Brustein begins by writing 'Of all the superfluous non-books being published this winter for the Christmas luxury trade, there is none more demoralizingly significant than a monster volume called *Nothing Personal*'.[68] The book, originally published in an oversize format, contains a lyrical essay by Baldwin and photographs by Richard Avedon, his old high-school friend and a successful fashion photographer. And while Baldwin is often depicted as a solitary artist, an image he possibly cultivated to deflect attention from his love life, the book is a reminder that he collaborated on several projects, including a lengthy taped conversation with the renowned sociologist Margaret Mead which became the book *A Rap on Race* (1971). He also worked with the French artist Yoran Cazac, whose striking watercolours enriched Baldwin's children's book, *Little Man Little Man: A Story of Childhood* (1976); Baldwin privately referred to Cazac as his wife. And towards the end of his life Baldwin collaborated on *A Lover's Question*, an experimental jazz album with Belgian-born musician David Linx, which features spoken-word contributions from the writer, along with a haunting rendition of the gospel song 'Take My Hand, Precious Lord'.

Nothing Personal was not Baldwin's first collaboration with a photographer. In the mid-1940s he met Theodore ('Teddy') Pelatowski, a photographer with whom he fell in love and who became the inspiration for the character Joey in *Giovanni's Room*. The aspiring writer and budding photographer embarked on a study of Harlem storefront churches. The proposed book, *Unto the Dying Lamb*, did not find a publisher, but remnants of the project remain, consisting of Pelatowski's photographs of young worshippers accompanied by Baldwin's stories about his religious upbringing.

The glossily produced *Nothing Personal* was a very different creature. A meditation on American culture – including the Civil Rights Movement, the counterculture and old Hollywood – the book includes photographs of Marilyn Monroe, a former enslaved person, a naked and hairy Allen Ginsberg and portraits of nameless patients from a psychiatric unit. The eclecticism and composition of the portraits did not appeal to Brustein, who complained that Avedon's subjects are rendered 'repulsive knaves, fools, and lunatics', with Baldwin 'interrupting from time to time, like a punchy and pugnacious drunk awakening from a boozy doze during a stag movie, to introduce his garrulous, irrelevant, and by now predictable comments on how to live, how to love, and how to build Jerusalem'.[69] Baldwin, Brustein complained, 'is now part and parcel of the very things he is criticizing', a damning indictment of a writer who had started to gain international visibility at the age of forty.[70]

Brustein's dismissal of *Nothing Personal* is a reminder that Baldwin, who is now the subject of near uniform adulation, was frequently pilloried during his career, from the right and the left, and from white and Black writers and critics. The literary critic Irving Howe bemoaned Baldwin's 'rifts in logic' and the African American academic Harold Cruse complained of the 'tormented inconsistency that runs through Mr. Baldwin's work', while the Black American writer Albert Murray referred to the 'exasperating confusion' in his writing.[71] Baldwin was accused of being a polemicist, rather than a nuanced novelist, but he was also the subject of *ad hominem* attacks from peers, critics and the Federal Bureau of Investigation, which was uncomfortable with his sexuality. J. Edgar Hoover, the FBI's long-serving director, greenlit surveillance on Baldwin from the early 1960s, which resulted in a dossier that ran to nearly 1,800 pages. 'Isn't Baldwin a well known pervert[?]' the FBI director scrawled in the margins of one file, believing that the Bureau's reports would never be declassified. Another FBI file reads 'It has been heard that BALDWIN may be a homosexual and he appeared as if he may be one' – one of many examples in which surveillance and gossip are entangled in a tight embrace.[72] Hoover and the Bureau were by no means unique in their discomfort with Baldwin's sexuality. Martin Luther King Jr., who was subjected to blackmail by the FBI surrounding his alleged extramarital affairs, was worried about having Baldwin too close to the Civil Rights Movement lest his sexuality taint the cause.

There's a book waiting to be written about Baldwin's famous detractors, from Norman Mailer and Eldridge Cleaver to Philip Roth. In his review of Baldwin's *Blues for Mister*

Charlie (1964), a play based on the last days of Emmett Till, a Black teenager who was brutally murdered in 1955, Roth, the author of *American Pastoral* and *Portnoy's Complaint*, criticised what he termed Baldwin's 'sentimentalizing of masculinity', arguing that the play 'is a soap opera designed to illustrate the superiority of blacks over whites'.[73] Baldwin's characters, Roth claimed, were little more than Black American caricatures who 'dance better' and whose 'penises are longer, or stiffer'. Mario Puzo, the screenwriter and novelist, best known for his bestselling novel *The Godfather* (1969), panned *Tell Me How Long the Train's Been Gone* (1968), calling it a 'one dimensional novel with mostly cardboard characters'.[74] And Puzo was not alone: the *New York Times* critic called the novel 'a disaster in virtually every particular – theme, characterization, plot, rhetoric'.[75] And while *Another Country* was Baldwin's most commercially successful novel, its descriptions of sex troubled readers, including the African American writer Eugenia W. Collier, who concluded that Baldwin's novel has, 'as the cliché says, something for everyone – in this instance, something offensive for everyone'.[76] Many readers, including Hoover, were appalled at the graphic descriptions of sex, while others were bemused by the lack of a clear political message, as well as the uneven writing. Augusta Strong, reviewing *Another Country* in *Freedomways*, a leading African American political and cultural journal of the 1960s, concluded that it is 'a novel that those who have admired his earlier work must find bafflingly inexpert and disappointing'.[77]

The graphic sex scenes in *Another Country* were bound to ruffle some moral feathers in the early 1960s. And it is certainly the case that many readers and critics were deeply uncomfortable with Baldwin's sexuality. But it would be remiss to overlook the ways in which Baldwin often failed to live up to the frequently hagiographic accounts that have stacked up in recent years. Baldwin is today known for his progressive and even radical outlook, but he was at times out of step with younger female writers and activists. 'Look, if we're living in the same house and you're my wife or my woman, I have to be responsible for that house', Baldwin told Nikki Giovanni, a line which did not go down well. 'I can get my own damn steak', Giovanni told Baldwin.[78]

Giovanni's Room is rightly celebrated as an early and pioneering novel about love between two men, but the descriptions of women make for uncomfortable reading and there is something bordering on disgust in the descriptions of a cross-dresser whom David meets in a bar – 'It looked like a mummy or a zombie – this was the first, overwhelming impression – of something walking after it had been put to death' – just as there are descriptions in a later novel of 'the broken down British faggot' and 'the faggot painter and his lesbian wife'.[79]

Baldwin also courted controversy with his writing, at times cloddish, about Black–Jewish relations. In an early essay, 'The Harlem Ghetto' (1948), he explained that 'The Negro, facing a Jew, hates, at bottom, not his Jewishness but the color of his skin'.[80] After the publication of his provocative essay 'Negroes Are Anti-Semitic Because They're Anti-White' in 1967 and an article published the same year in *Freedomways* called 'Anti-Semitism and Black Power', Baldwin had to defend himself against charges of antisemitism. In his 1970 essay for the *New York Review of Books*, 'An Open Letter to My Sister, Angela Davis', Baldwin described the activist, author and academic as a 'Jewish housewife in the boxcar headed for Dachau', which kickstarted a heated public debate with Shlomo Katz, editor of *Midstream*, an intellectual Zionist journal. In open letters, Katz took Baldwin to task for comparing Davis's experience to that of Holocaust victims.

During a career that spanned four decades, Baldwin rarely played it safe and he got things wrong. He acknowledged that as a 'perfectly impossible man' his work left him open to 'a vast amount of misunderstanding', a reminder that he did not expect to be sanitised, or for his faults to be airbrushed out.[81] Rather, his work demands critical attention, even – and especially – when it is troubling, contradictory and disturbing, which is something I have thought deeply about as I write about my father. As I reflect on my father's contradictions and mistakes, a fuller picture of him emerges, which I need to hang on to as his emaciated body withers and his sense of the world diminishes.

Epilogue

Thou poor ghost

Above all, we cannot not live in the present. He is blessed above all mortals who loses no moment of the passing life in remembering the past.

Henry David Thoreau, 'Walking' (1862)

When I write I have trouble with my tenses. Where I was tomorrow is where I am today, where I would be yesterday.

Alexander Trocchi, *Cain's Book* (1960)

For several weeks, I have been waking up at 4.44 each morning after a recurring dream in which my father telephones me. Before his illness we did not phone each other regularly, but when it felt right we would chat for an hour or more at a time about literature, family and cricket. In my dream, my father's voice was assured; he spoke with his customary warmth and humour and assured me that he was feeling much better. When I awake each morning at the same time, I lie in the darkness trying to slip back into the warmth of that dream, which I never quite manage, waiting for the glooming peace of morning to arrive.

In many ways, my recurring dream is not surprising. I've been devouring articles and books on Alzheimer's, a topic which seems to be in the news more frequently, although that may be only because I am so keenly aware of it. A recent *World Alzheimer Report* estimates that there are 50 million people living with dementia globally, with someone developing dementia every three seconds. By 2050, an estimated 150 million people will be living with this disease, a silent pandemic that also diminishes the quality of life for many carers.[1] And while around 150 drugs are currently being tested in clinical trials, most of these aim only to slow down the progression of the disease, and no cure has yet been found. *King Lear* captures many of the devastating hallmarks of Alzheimer's. 'Who is it that can tell me who I am?', is reminiscent of the harrowing response uttered by Auguste Deter – 'I have lost myself' – while the Fool's reply, 'Lear's shadow', captures the language of spectres and ghosts that haunts those with the disease. In Shakespeare's play, however, Lear recovers his senses, something that has yet to happen, the promise of drug companies notwithstanding.

Three drugs (donanemab, lecanemab and remternetug) have had promising results, but only with early-stage Alzheimer's sufferers. The aim of the drugs is to break down the amyloid plaques in the brains of people living with the disease. Most immunotherapies, as these drugs are called, require patients to visit clinics, where they are hooked up to an intravenous drip. Injections are being trialled. These drugs do not tackle the root cause of the disease; rather they slow down the effects of Alzheimer's, but they cannot stop its insidious intent. Even prolonged treatment over many months might serve to decelerate the progress of the disease only modestly. In the UK, finding a drug that can impede the disease is complicated by poor records of diagnosis in some parts of the country. Less than half of the UK is on track to meet the government's dementia diagnosis rate of 66.7 per cent by April 2024, so the chances of receiving an early diagnosis come down simply to where you live. Recent figures estimate that 40 per cent of people aged sixty-five and over thought to be living with dementia do not have a diagnosis, a figure the *Guardian* puts at 115,000.[2] Those that are diagnosed at a later stage are less likely to see the benefits of new drugs, or to take part in clinical trials.

The importance of scientific developments in the treatment of Alzheimer's notwithstanding, I am not a scientist, nor was I meant to be. I find myself wondering whether writing about my father's condition is an act of love or an act of betrayal. This is the first book I've written that he cannot read; I feel a burden of responsibility – as well as a guilty sense of freedom – because my father cannot respond to what I have written. In a thoughtful article published in the *New Yorker* in 2014, Stefan Merrill Block ponders his future in the knowledge of his family's predisposition to Alzheimer's. 'I'm left with urgent questions that only fiction can answer', he writes. 'What do those late stages *feel* like? What is it like to lose oneself and still live? Could there be some essential kernel of selfhood that survives until the end? Mid- to late-stage sufferers, lost in their aphasia, can't explain it to us.'[3] Block's article raises important questions about the role that art can play in the portrayal of Alzheimer's. *Still Alice*, a novel by Lisa Genova – which has been made into a film starring Julianne Moore – tells the story of Alice Howland, a linguistics professor at Columbia University who is diagnosed with early-onset Alzheimer's shortly after her fiftieth birthday. As Genova explained in an interview, echoing Block's belief in fiction's ability to map the unknown, 'The thing I needed to know the most was what does it feel like to have

[Alzheimer's] and I couldn't get an answer to that question in anything I read'.[4] Block's debut novel, *The Story of Forgetting* (2008), imagines Alzheimer's as a familial curse over the course of 400 years. In a parallel universe called Isidora, memory carries no importance; the inhabitants live in a perpetual cycle of newness without the burden of remembering.

There are numerous novels that tackle the subject of Alzheimer's, including two major works published in 2014: Matthew Thomas's magisterial – and very long – *We Are not Ourselves*, which tracks one family over three generations and which pays sensitive attention to the pain experienced by carers; and Emma Healey's bestselling *Elizabeth Is Missing*, in which Maud, an elderly lady living with dementia, attempts to solve the mystery of her missing friend, an event she confuses with the disappearance of her sister decades earlier. As the literary critic Pieter Vermeulen has pointed out in an astute analysis of dementia in contemporary literature and theory, literary studies have 'the resources to attend to the repetitions, reductions, indirections and fragmentations that mark the language of dementia', which carries echoes of the hallmarks of modernist literature. But on the other hand, as Vermeulen observes, cultural representations of dementia are 'linked to a paradoxical ability to see darkness and thus to witness the truth'.[5] In the case of my father, I cling onto a hope, almost religious in its fervour, that his enigmatic utterances are emanating from his distilled, unfettered self, but my faith is receding. All I know is that I cannot be certain about what my father thinks, sees or feels; his mind has become, to me at least, an incomprehensible map of a world in which there may be dragons.

A few months ago my mother called me to say that she had been arranging my father's funeral. Like Shakespeare's notion of the seven acts of life in *As You Like It*, the degeneration of Alzheimer's disease is measured in seven stages. My father is almost certainly at the seventh stage, so is unlikely to live for more than a year or so. My mother tells me that she does not wish to burden me with writing my father's eulogy and that she has asked ones of his former friends, a colleague. When she visits, she brings a small bundle of my father's clothes, including a jumper, shirt and pyjamas for me to keep. For weeks I cannot bear to open the bag, which gathers dust in the corner of my bedroom.

On holiday in Sicily, where I have been finishing this book, I find myself drawn to the prayer candles in the baroque majesty of the Chiesa di San Giovanni Evangelista in Scicli, a church that would have fascinated my father. I place some money into the donation box, pressing the button on the electric candle as I utter a prayer of sorts to my father, whose jumper I realise I am wearing. The candle does not light up, a moment which seems narratively right. I am distracted from my thoughts by the squeals of laughter that come from my two daughters, grandchildren my father will never meet, a man, like the old writer in William S. Burroughs's *The Western Lands*, 'who had reached the end of words, the end of what can be done with words'.[6]

Acknowledgements

The idea for this book came to me after my second whisky (Johnnie Walker Black Label) at a hotel bar in Leuven, Belgium, in May 2020. I would like to thank the bar staff for looking after me. I was in Leuven to give a talk on James Baldwin at Leuven KU University, where I sounded out the idea to my hosts, Pieter Vermeulen and Remo Verdickt. My father had recently moved into a care home and his presence – and absence – was keenly felt. I am grateful to both for offering their input, along with Pieter's insightful work on Dementia Studies, as well as Remo's generosity in sharing his impressive research. I would also like to thank Catharine Morris and Robert Potts at the *Times Literary Supplement*, who responded positively to my pitch for a freelance piece on James Baldwin and my father, which sowed the seeds for this book. The article was published as 'Be with Me a Little Longer' (*TLS*, 2 September 2022). I am particularly grateful to my friend and colleague Natalie Zacek for reading a draft of this book, and for her insightful suggestions, and to the anonymous reader for thorough comments and corrections. Thank you to Sam Thozer and Magdelena Mullerova for reading the book proof. I am grateful for permission to use a quotation for the epigraph to Chapter 1 from W. H. Auden's *The Sea and the Mirror*, copyright 1944 and © renewed 1972 by W. H. Auden; from *Collected Poems* by W. H. Auden, edited by Edward Mendelson (New York: Random House, 1976), p. 312. Used by permission of Random House, an imprint and division of Penguin Random House LLC. All rights reserved. Copyright © 1947 by W. H. Auden. Reprinted by permission of Curtis Brown, Ltd. All rights reserved.

I would not – and could not – have written this book without the trust and support of my mother and three sisters, who have visited my father while I have written about him. This book was written during a period of some upheaval: moving house four times within a year, several months of travelling, as well as the birth of my fifth child. I am grateful to JJ, for entertaining my youngest children while I wrote this book, and to my wife and children, who, for many months, mistook my face for a laptop. My oldest three children – Sonny, Wilf and Monty – knew and adored my father, which helped me to complete this book. Delilah and Goldie, I hope, will be inspired by their grandfather, even if they did not meet him.

My wife, Ellie, has offered thoughtful comments through-out, as well as driving me to visit my father. I am grateful to friends for their sensitive and insightful suggestions, among them Horatio Clare, Rebecca Shooter, Dan Tang and Matt Heath. Conversations with Zaffar Kunial helped me think through complex aspects of Baldwin's life and work. At Manchester University Press I have been lucky to work with a team of brilliant and sensitive editors, including Kim Walker and Dave Watkins. I am grateful to Kim for persuading me to write this book during a difficult time, and to Alun Richards for his support. I am particularly grateful to Ralph Footring for his sharp eye and quick responses during the copy-editing and proofing of the book. I have been fortunate to be part of a large transnational community of scholars and writers who share my passion for James Baldwin's work. Thank you to my friend and co-editor of *James Baldwin Review*, Justin A. Joyce, as well as James Campbell, whose sharp eye and generosity have sustained my interest in Baldwin for over twenty years.

Finally, I am grateful to the team of carers at my father's home in North Shropshire, whose affection for my father has ushered in spring during the dark days of winter.

Notes

Prologue: If we are not ourselves, who are we?

1 Georges Perec, 'Preamble', in *Life: A User's Manual*, translated by David Bellos (London: Harvill, 1987), p. xv.

2 Joan Didion, *The White Album* (New York: Pocket Books, 1979), p. 11.

3 John McCrae, 'In Flanders Fields' (1915), https://www.poetryfoundation.org/poems/47380/in-flanders-fields (accessed 21 May 2024).

4 Perec, *Life: A User's Manual*, p. 497.

5 James Baldwin, 'Autobiographical Notes', in *Collected Essays*, edited by Toni Morrison (New York: Library of America, 1998), p. 9.

6 Baldwin's first essay, as opposed to reviews and review essays, was 'Harlem Ghetto', published in *Commentary* magazine, February 1948. 'Everybody's Protest Novel' might be considered his first major essay.

7 James Baldwin, 'Everybody's Protest Novel', in *Collected Essays*, p. 11.

8 Baldwin, 'Everybody's Protest Novel', p. 18.

9 Baldwin, 'Everybody's Protest Novel', p. 15.

10 James Baldwin, 'Telling Talk from a Negro Writer', *Life*, 24 May 1963, p. 89.

11 Baldwin, 'Everybody's Protest Novel', p. 15.

12 James Baldwin, 'A Fly in Buttermilk', in *Collected Essays*, p. 191.

13 James Baldwin, 'A Talk to Teachers', in *Collected Essays*, p. 681.

14 Baldwin, 'A Talk to Teachers', p. 679.

15 Baldwin, 'A Talk to Teachers', p. 678.

16 Baldwin, 'A Talk to Teachers', p. 679.

17 David Leeming, *James Baldwin: A Biography* (New York: Arcade Publishing, 2015), p. 14.
18 Sophia Gardner and Talia Heisey, 'James Baldwin's Years at UMass and the Five Colleges', https://www.umass.edu/diversity/blackpresence/james-baldwins-years-umass (accessed 21 May 2024).
19 Gardner and Heisey, 'James Baldwin's Years at UMass and the Five Colleges'.
20 Leeming, *James Baldwin: A Biography*, p. 340.
21 James Baldwin, 'Dark Days', in *Collected Essays*, p. 788.
22 Michele Elam, 'Review of New York City's "The Year of Baldwin"', *James Baldwin Review*, vol. 1 (2015), pp. 202–3.
23 Christina Davis, 'Interview with Toni Morrison', *Présence Africaine*, vol. 145 (1988), p. 142.
24 James Baldwin, 'Many Thousands Gone', in *Collected Essays*, p. 22.
25 James Baldwin, 'The White Man's Guilt', in *Collected Essays*, pp. 722–3.
26 James Baldwin, *The Fire Next Time*, in *Collected Essays*, p. 294.
27 James Baldwin, 'Stranger in the Village', in *Collected Essays*, p. 119.
28 Toni Morrison, *Beloved* (New York: Plume, 1987), p. 73.
29 Toni Morrison, 'I Wanted to Carve Out a World Both Culture Specific and Race-Free', *Guardian*, 8 August 2019, https://www.theguardian.com/books/2019/aug/08/toni-morrison-rememory-essay (accessed 21 May 2024).
30 James Baldwin, *The Evidence of Things Not Seen* (New York: Henry Holt, 1995), pp. xiii–xv.
31 Baldwin, 'The White Man's Guilt', p. 723.
32 Morrison, 'I Wanted to Carve Out a World'.
33 James Baldwin, *No Name in the Street*, in *Collected Essays*, p. 365.
34 All quotes in this paragraph from Baldwin, *No Name in the Street*, p. 383.
35 James Baldwin, 'Princes and Powers', in *Collected Essays*, p. 143.
36 Baldwin, *No Name in the Street*, p. 383
37 Baldwin, *No Name in the Street*, p. 435.
38 Baldwin, *No Name in the Street*, p. 353.
39 Eddie Glaude Jr., 'How James Baldwin's Faulty Memory Yielded Lasting Truth', *Daily Beast*, 4 July 2020, https://www.thedailybeast.com/how-james-baldwins-faulty-memory-yielded-lasting-truth (accessed 21 May 2024).
40 Baldwin, *The Evidence of Things Not Seen*, p. xii.
41 Philip Roth, *Patrimony: A True Story* (New York: Simon & Schuster, 1991), p. 74.
42 Figures respectively from Alzheimer's Society, 'How Many People Have Dementia in the UK?', https://www.alzheimers.org.uk/blog/

how-many-people-have-dementia-uk, and https://www.alz.org/alzheimers-dementia/facts-figures (accessed 21 May 2024).

43 See James C. Harris, 'Pinel Delivering the Insane', *Archives of General Psychiatry*, vol. 60, no. 6 (2003), p. 552.
44 For a translation of Alzheimer's pioneering paper on the eponymous disease originally published in 1907, see *Clinical Anatomy*, vol. 8, no. 6 (1995), pp. 429–31. All quotations used in my book are taken from this translation, unless referenced otherwise.
45 David Shenk, *The Forgetting* (London: Flamingo, 2003), p. 24.
46 Susan Sontag, *AIDS and Its Metaphors* (London: Penguin, 2009), p. 124.
47 Sontag, *AIDS and Its Metaphors*, p. 15.
48 See Barry Reisberg et al., 'Retrogenesis: Clinical, Physiologic, and Pathologic Mechanisms in Brain Aging, Alzheimer's and Other Dementing Processes', *European Archives of Psychiatry and Clinical Neuroscience*, vol. 249 (February 1999), pp. 28–36.
49 Sontag, *AIDS and Its Metaphors*, p. 6.
50 Rodrigo Quian Quiroga, *The Forgetting Machine: Memory, Perception, and the 'Jennifer Aniston Neuron'* (Dallas: BenBella Books, 2017), p. 12.
51 Cited by Quiroga, *The Forgetting Machine*, p. 139.
52 Shenk, *The Forgetting*, p. 16.
53 Cited by Shenk, *The Forgetting*, pp. 44–5.
54 Quiroga, *The Forgetting Machine*, p. 17.
55 William James, *The Principles of Psychology* (1890), ch. 7, https://psychclassics.yorku.ca/James/Principles/prin16.htm (accessed 21 May 2024).
56 Shenk, *The Forgetting*, p. 56.
57 James Baldwin, *Giovanni's Room*, in *Early Novels and Short Stories* (New York: Library of America, 1998), p. 294.
58 Mike Doherty, 'Will Self on the Literary Novel's Demise, and Why Naomi Klein Won't Fix the World', *Maclean's*, 16 January 2018, https://macleans.ca/culture/books/will-self-on-the-literary-novels-demise-and-why-naomi-klein-wont-fix-the-world (accessed 21 May 2024).
59 Rebecca Solnit, *Wanderlust: A History of Walking* (London: Granta, 2002), p. xv.
60 Henry David Thoreau, *Walking* (New York: Dover, 2019), p. 21.
61 Cited by Solnit, *Wanderlust*, p. 14.
62 Jack Kerouac, *The Dharma Bums* (London: Penguin, 2007), p. 66.
63 Walt Whitman, 'As I Walk, Solitary, Unattended', https://whitmanarchive.org/item/ppp.00473_00702 (accessed 21 May 2024).
64 Baldwin, *No Name in the Street*, p. 392.
65 Baldwin, *No Name in the Street*, p. 450.

66 Baldwin uses this song as an epitaph to his essay 'The Black Boy Looks at the White Boy', in *Collected Essays*, p. 269.

Chapter 1: Fathers and illness

1 James Baldwin, 'Notes of a Native Son', in *Collected Essays*, edited by Toni Morrison (New York: Library of America, 1998), p. 63.

2 Baldwin, 'Notes of a Native Son', p. 63.

3 Baldwin, 'Notes of a Native Son', p. 66.

4 Baldwin, 'Notes of a Native Son', p. 66.

5 Baldwin, 'Notes of a Native Son', p. 66.

6 For one of the few accounts of Berdis, see Anna Malaika Tubbs, *The Three Mothers: How the Mothers of Martin Luther King, Jr., Malcolm X, and James Baldwin Shaped a Nation* (New York: Flatiron Books, 2021).

7 James Baldwin, *No Name in the Street*, in *Collected Essays*, p. 395.

8 James Baldwin, 'A Fly in Buttermilk', in *Collected Essays*, p. 187; Baldwin, *No Name in the Street*, p. 386.

9 Baldwin, *No Name in the Street*, p. 353.

10 Baldwin, *No Name in the Street*, p. 353.

11 Baldwin, *No Name in the Street*, p. 353.

12 James Baldwin, 'Autobiographical Notes', in *Collected Essays*, p. 5.

13 Baldwin, 'Autobiographical Notes', p. 5.

14 James Baldwin, 'Freaks and the American Ideal of Manhood', in *Collected Essays*, p. 817.

15 James Baldwin, 'Equal in Paris', in *Collected Essays*, p. 112.

16 Baldwin, *No Name in the Street*, p. 354.

17 David Leeming, *James Baldwin: A Biography* (New York: Arcade Publishing, 2015), p. 21.

18 Karen Thorsen (director), *James Baldwin: The Price of the Ticket* (Nobody Knows Productions, 1989).

19 Thorsen, *James Baldwin: The Price of the Ticket*.

20 Thorsen, *James Baldwin: The Price of the Ticket*.

21 Leslie Bennetts, 'James Baldwin Reflects on "Go Tell It" PBS Film', *New York Times*, 10 January 1985, https://www.nytimes.com/1985/01/10/books/james-baldwin-reflects-on-go-tell-it-pbs-film.html (accessed 22 May 2024).

22 Baldwin, 'Notes of a Native Son', p. 68.

23 Baldwin, 'Autobiographical Notes', p. 5.

24 James Baldwin, *The Fire Next Time*, in *Collected Essays*, p. 298. Within this book, the n-word appears twice in quotations and three

times to reference the title of a film. The quotations and titles have not been altered, in order both to preserve the material specificity of the original context and to reflect Baldwin's use of the word, which he employed to draw attention to the dehumanising effects of racism during his lifetime.

25 Baldwin, 'Notes of a Native Son', p. 80.

26 Baldwin, 'Notes of a Native Son', p. 63.

27 William S. Burroughs, *Junky: The Definitive Text of 'Junk'*, edited and introduced by Oliver Harris (New York: Penguin, 2003), p. 77.

28 James Baldwin, 'The Death of the Prophet', in *The Cross of Redemption: Uncollected Writings*, edited and introduced by Randall Kenan (New York: Pantheon Books, 2010), p. 358.

29 Baldwin, 'The Death of the Prophet', p. 358.

30 T. S. Eliot, 'The Hollow Men', taken from *Collected Poems, 1909–1962* (New York: Harcourt, Brace & World, 1963), p. 81. © T. S. Eliot and reprinted by permission of Faber & Faber Ltd.

31 Baldwin, 'The Death of the Prophet', p. 364.

32 Baldwin, *No Name in the Street*, pp. 353–4.

33 Baldwin, *No Name in the Street*, p. 354.

34 Avery Gordon, *Ghostly Matters: Haunting and the Sociological Imagination* (Minneapolis: University of Minnesota Press, 1997), p. xvi.

35 See Jacques Derrida, *Specters of Marx: The State of the Debt, the Work of Mourning and the New International* (London: Routledge, 2006).

36 Mark Fisher, 'What Is Hauntology?', *Film Quarterly*, vol. 66, no. 1 (2012), p. 16.

37 James Baldwin, *Go Tell It on the Mountain* (London: Penguin, 1991), pp. 20, 21.

38 Harold Norse, *Memoirs of a Bastard Angel* (which has a preface by James Baldwin) (New York: William Morrow & Co., 1989), p. 114.

39 Cited by W. J. Weatherby, *James Baldwin: Artist on Fire* (London: Michael Joseph, 1990), p. 96.

40 Leeming, *James Baldwin*, p. 112.

41 James Baldwin, 'The Outing', in *Going to Meet the Man* (London: Penguin, 1991), p. 39.

42 Baldwin, *Go Tell It on the Mountain*, p. 20.

43 1 Samuel 18: 1–2 and 2 Samuel 1: 26.

44 1 Samuel 20: 30–3.

45 Jordan Elgrably and George Plimpton, 'The Art of Fiction LXXVIII: James Baldwin', in *Conversations with James Baldwin*, edited by Fred R. Standley and Louis H. Pratt (Jackson: University Press of Mississippi, 1989), p. 239.

46 James Baldwin, 'Preservation of Innocence', in *Collected Essays*, p. 600.
47 James Baldwin, 'Freaks and the American Ideal of Manhood', in *Collected Essays*, pp. 819, 821.
48 Baldwin, 'Freaks and the American Ideal of Manhood', p. 818.
49 Baldwin, 'Freaks and the American Ideal of Manhood', p. 818.
50 James Baldwin, 'Introduction', in *The Price of the Ticket: Collected Nonfiction, 1948–1985* (New York: St Martin's Press, 1985), p. xii.
51 James Baldwin, 'The New Lost Generation', in *The Price of the Ticket*, p. 305.
52 Baldwin, 'The New Lost Generation', p. 659.
53 Baldwin, 'The New Lost Generation', p 661.
54 James Baldwin, 'This Evening, This Morning, So Soon', in *Going to Meet the Man*, p. 163.
55 Baldwin, 'The New Lost Generation', p. 661.
56 Baldwin, 'The New Lost Generation', p. 661.
57 Langston Hughes, 'Suicide's Note', https://www.poetryfoundation.org/poems/147906/suicide39s-note (accessed 24 May 2024). Used by permission of International Literary Properties (ILP).
58 James Baldwin, 'The Price of the Ticket', in *Collected Essays*, p. 830.
59 Baldwin, 'The Price of the Ticket', p. 830.
60 Baldwin, 'The Price of the Ticket', p. 831.
61 David Leeming, *Amazing Grace: A Life of Beauford Delaney* (New York: Oxford University Press, 1998), p. 64.
62 Baldwin, 'On the Painter Beauford Delaney', in *Collected Essays*, p. 720.
63 Baldwin, *Go Tell It on the Mountain*, p. 227.
64 Leeming, *Amazing Grace: A Life of Beauford Delaney*, pp. 125, 127.
65 Leeming, *Amazing Grace: A Life of Beauford Delaney*, p. 191.
66 Leeming, *Amazing Grace: A Life of Beauford Delaney*, p. 196.
67 Leeming, *Amazing Grace: A Life of Beauford Delaney*, p. 198.

Chapter 2: Writing home

1 Michael Anderson, 'Trapped Inside James Baldwin', *New York Times*, 29 March 1998, p. 13, https://www.nytimes.com/1998/03/29/books/trapped-inside-james-baldwin.html (accessed 24 May 2024).
2 Amiri Baraka, *Eulogies* (New York: Marisilio Publishers, 1996), p. 95.
3 Anon., 'Nation: The Root of the Negro Problem', *Time*, 17 May 1963, https://time.com/archive/6626512/nation-the-root-of-the-negro-problem (accessed 24 May 2024).

4 'The Black Scholar Interviews James Baldwin', in *Conversations with James Baldwin*, edited by Fred R. Standley and Louis H. Pratt (Jackson: University of Mississippi Press, 1989), p. 154.

5 Caryl Phillips, 'James Baldwin: The Price of the Ticket (2007)', in *Color Me English: Migration and Belonging Before and After 9/11* (New York: The New Press, 2011), p. 246.

6 James Baldwin, 'The Discovery of What It Means to Be an American', in *Collected Essays*, edited by Toni Morrison (New York: Library of America, 1998), p. 142.

7 See the Designation Report, 'James Baldwin Residence', Landmarks Preservation Commission, 18 June 2019, https://www.nyclgbtsites. org/wp-content/uploads/2019/06/James-Baldwin-Residence.pdf (accessed 24 May 2024).

8 James Baldwin, 'Architectural Digest Visits: James Baldwin', *Architectural Digest*, August 1987, pp. 121–2.

9 Karen Thorsen (director), *James Baldwin: The Price of the Ticket* (Nobody Knows Productions, 1989).

10 Toni Morrison, 'The Site of Memory', in *Inventing the Truth: The Art and Craft of Memoir*, 2nd edition, edited by William Zinsser (Boston: Houghton Mifflin, 1995), p. 92.

11 Angela Cobbina, 'Blues for Mr. Baldwin', in *Conversations with James Baldwin*, p. 256.

12 Ida Lewis, 'Ida Lewis and James Baldwin', in *Conversations with James Baldwin*, p. 83.

13 Thorsen, *James Baldwin: The Price of the Ticket*.

14 James Baldwin, 'Notes of a Native Son', in *Collected Essays*, p. 83.

15 James Baldwin, *The Fire Next Time*, in *Collected Essays*, p. 294.

16 Baldwin, *The Fire Next Time*, p. 294.

17 James Baldwin, *No Name in the Street*, in *Collected Essays*, p. 475.

18 Baldwin, *The Fire Next Time*, p. 340.

19 Horace Ové (director), *Baldwin's Nigger* (Infilms, 1969).

20 Ové, *Baldwin's Nigger*.

21 James Baldwin, 'Encounter on the Seine: Black Meets Brown', in *Collected Essays*, p. 86.

22 Baldwin, 'Encounter on the Seine', p. 89.

23 Harold R. Isaacs, 'Five Writers and Their African Ancestors. Part II', *Phylon*, vol. 21, no. 4 (1960), p. 324.

24 James Baldwin, 'Princes and Powers', in *Collected Essays*, p. 148.

25 Baldwin, 'Princes and Powers', p. 148.

26 Baldwin, 'Princes and Powers', p. 146.

27 Baldwin, 'Princes and Powers', p. 152.

28 Baldwin, 'Princes and Powers', p. 153.

29 François Bondy, 'James Baldwin, as Interviewed by François Bondy', *Transition*, no. 12 (January–February 1964), p. 16.

30 David Leeming, *James Baldwin: A Biography* (New York: Alfred A. Knopf, 2004), p. 207.

31 James Baldwin, 'Letters from a Journey', in *Soon, One Morning: New Writings by American Negroes, 1940–62*, edited by Herbert Hill (New York: Alfred A. Knopf, 1966), p. 40; Leeming, *James Baldwin: A Biography*, p. 181.

32 James Campbell, *Talking at the Gates: A Life of James Baldwin* (Edinburgh: Polygon, 2021), p. 64.

33 James Baldwin, 'The Discovery of What It Means to Be an American', in *Collected Essays*, p. 138.

34 Magdalena Zaborowska, *James Baldwin's Turkish Decade: Erotics of Exile* (Durham: Duke University Press, 2009), p. 1.

35 Isaacs, 'Five Writers and Their African Ancestors. Part II', p. 323.

36 Baldwin, 'Notes of a Native Son', p. 70.

37 Baldwin, 'Notes of a Native Son', p. 71.

38 Baldwin, *No Name in the Street*, pp. 394, 395.

39 Baldwin, *No Name in the Street*, p. 397.

40 James Baldwin, 'Stranger in the Village', in *Collected Essays*, p. 118.

41 Baldwin, 'Stranger in the Village', p. 121.

42 Addison Gayle Jr., 'The Function of Black Literature at the Present Time', in *The Black Aesthetic*, edited by Addison Gayle Jr. (New York: Doubleday and Company, 1971), pp. 389, 390.

43 James Baldwin, 'Autobiographical Notes', in *Collected Essays*, p. 8.

44 Baldwin, 'Stranger in the Village', p. 129.

45 Jordan Elgrably and George Plimpton, 'The Art of Fiction LXXVIII: James Baldwin', in *Conversations with James Baldwin*, edited by Fred R. Standley and Louis H. Pratt (Jackson: University Press of Mississippi, 1989), p. 239.

46 Pierre Nora, 'Between Memory and History: Les Lieux de Mémoire', *Representations*, no. 26, special issue: *Memory and CounterMemory* (spring 1989), p. 12.

47 Untitled poem from 1956 by Allen Ginsberg taken from Allen Ginsberg and Peter Orlovsky, *Straight Hearts' Delight: Love Poems and Selected Letters, 1947–1980* (San Francisco: Gay Sunshine Press), p. 139. Copyright © 1956, Allen Ginsberg LLC, used by permission of The Wylie Agency (UK) Limited.

48 James Baldwin and Sol Stein, *Native Sons* (New York: One World, 2004), p. 87.

49 'A Kumquat for John Keats' taken from Tony Harrison, *Collected Poems* (London: Penguin, 2007), pp. 221, 220, 221. ©Tony Harrison and reprinted by permission of Faber & Faber Ltd.

50 James Baldwin, 'Everybody's Protest Novel', in *Collected Essays*, p. 15.
51 D. Quentin Miller, *A Criminal Power: James Baldwin and the Law* (Columbus: Ohio State University Press, 2012), p. 12.
52 James Baldwin, *Giovanni's Room*, in *Early Novels and Stories* (New York: Library of America, 1998), p. 294.
53 James Baldwin, 'This Morning, This Evening, So Soon', in *Going to Meet the Man* (London: Penguin, 1991), p. 164.
54 James Baldwin, 'The Price of the Ticket', in *Collected Essays*, p. 841.
55 Baldwin, *Giovanni's Room*, p. 315.
56 Mircea Eliade, *The Sacred and the Profane: The Nature of Religion*, translated by William R. Trask (New York: Harvest, 1959), p. 64.
57 Lynn Casteel Harper, *On Vanishing: Mortality, Dementia, and What It Means to Disappear* (New York: Catapult, 2020), p. 148.
58 John Berger, 'The Meaning of Home', https://www.thoughtco.com/the-meaning-of-home-by-john-berger-1692267 (accessed 24 May 2024).

Chapter 3: Some who wander are lost

1 'William S. Burroughs, The Art of Fiction No. 36', interview by Conrad Knickerbocker, *Paris Review*, no. 35 (fall 1965), https://www.theparisreview.org/interviews/4424/the-art-of-fiction-no-36-william-s-burroughs (accessed 24 May 2024).
2 Jamie Wadhawan (director), *Cain's Film* (1969).
3 See Henry Louis Gates Jr., 'Introduction: "Tell Me, Sir ... What Is 'Black' Literature?"', *PMLA*, vol. 105, no. 1 (1990), pp. 11–22.
4 Stuart Jeffries, 'Britain's Most Racist Election: The Story of Smethwick, 50 Years On', *Guardian*, 15 October, 2014, https://www.theguardian.com/world/2014/oct/15/britains-most-racist-election-smethwick-50-years-on (accessed 27 May 2024).
5 Nicholas Buccola, *The Fire Is Upon Us: James Baldwin, William F. Buckley Jr., and the Debate over Race in America* (Princeton: Princeton University Press, 2019), p. 3.
6 Buccola, *The Fire Is Upon Us*, p. 892.
7 William F. Buckley, 'Why the South Must Prevail' (1957), https://adamgomez.files.wordpress.com/2012/03/whythesouthmustprevail-1957.pdf (accessed 27 May 2024).
8 The interview was published in the London *Sunday Times*, 4 March 1956, and in *The Reporter*, 22 March 1956.
9 James Baldwin, 'Faulkner and Desegregation', in *Collected Essays*, edited by Toni Morrison (New York: Library of America, 1998), p. 209.

10 James Baldwin, *The Fire Next Time*, in *Collected Essays*, p. 294.

11 Baldwin, *The Fire Next Time*, p. 294.

12 Buccola, *The Fire Is Upon Us*, p. 2.

13 James Truslow Adams, *The Epic of America* (1931), Faded Page eBook, https://www.fadedpage.com/showbook.php?pid=20220138 (accessed 27 May 2024).

14 Jack Kerouac, *The Dharma Bums* (London: Penguin Classics, 2007), p. 83.

15 Adams, *The Epic of America*.

16 Langston Hughes, 'Harlem' (1951), https://www.poetryfoundation.org/poems/46548/harlem (accessed 27 May 2024).

17 Baldwin, *The Fire Next Time*, p. 337.

18 Ta-Nehisi Coates, *Between the World and Me* (New York: Random House, 2015), p. 11.

19 James Baldwin, 'Everybody's Protest Novel', in *Collected Essays*, p. 16.

20 Baldwin, *The Fire Next Time*, p. 337.

21 Baldwin, *The Fire Next Time*, p. 337.

22 James Baldwin, 'The American Dream and the American Negro', in *Collected Essays*, p. 717.

23 Buccola, *The Fire Is Upon Us*, p. 246.

24 Buccola, *The Fire Is Upon Us*, p. 248.

25 Jordan Elgrably and George Plimpton, 'The Art of Fiction LXXVIII: James Baldwin', in *Conversations with James Baldwin*, edited by Fred R. Standley and Louis H. Pratt (Jackson: University Press of Mississippi, 1989), p. 234.

26 Fern Marja Eckman, *The Furious Passage of James Baldwin* (New York: M. Evans, 1966), pp. 168–9.

27 T. E. Cassidy, 'The Long Struggle', *Commonweal*, no. 58 (22 May 1953), p. 186.

28 James Baldwin, *Go Tell It on the Mountain* (London: Penguin, 1991), p. 21.

29 Hollie I. West, 'James Baldwin: The Fire Still Burns', *Washington Post*, 8 April 1979, https://www.washingtonpost.com/archive/lifestyle/1979/04/08/james-baldwin-the-fire-still-burns (accessed 27 May 2024).

30 Charles Poore, 'Hemingway's Quality Built on a Stern Apprenticeship', *New York Times*, 29 October 1954, https://archive.nytimes.com/www.nytimes.com/books/99/07/04/specials/hemingway-quality.html (accessed 27 May 2024).

31 James Baldwin, 'This Nettle, Danger ...', in *Collected Essays*, p. 687.

32 Baldwin, *The Fire Next Time*, p. 314.

33 Baldwin, *The Fire Next Time*, p. 331.

34 Baldwin, *The Fire Next Time*, pp. 293–4.

35 LeRoi Jones, *Home: Social Essays* (New Jersey: Ecco Press, 1998), p. 133.

36 Eldridge Cleaver, *Soul on Ice*, with an introduction by Maxwell Geismar (New York: Ramparts, 1968), p. 106.

37 Cleaver, *Soul on Ice*, p. 110.

38 Henry Louis Gates Jr., 'The Black Man's Burden', in *Fear of a Queer Planet: Queer Politics and Social Theory*, edited by Michael Warner (Minneapolis: University of Minnesota Press, 1993), p. 233.

39 James Baldwin, *No Name in the Street*, in *Collected Essays*, p. 459.

40 Baldwin, *No Name in the Street*, p. 472.

41 Baldwin, *No Name in the Street*, p. 472.

42 Baldwin, *No Name in the Street*, p. 363.

43 Baldwin, *No Name in the Street*, pp. 398–9.

44 Baldwin, *No Name in the Street*, p. 364.

45 Elgrably and Plimpton, 'The Art of Fiction LXXVIII: James Baldwin', p. 87.

46 Raoul Peck (director), *I Am Not Your Negro* (Velvet Film, Artémis Productions, Close Up Films, ARTE France, RTS, RTBF, Shelter Prod and ITVS, 2016).

47 James Baldwin, 'The Price of the Ticket', in *Collected Essays*, p. 841.

48 John Updike, 'Spirit of '76', in *Endpoint and Other Poems* (London: Penguin, 2009), p. 19.

49 Updike, 'Endpoint: March Birthday 2002, and After', in *Endpoint and Other Poems*, p. 3. 'Endpoint: March Birthday 2002, and After' and 'Endpoint: Spirit of '76' (above) both from *Endpoint and Other Poems* by John Updike, copyright © 2009 by The Estate of John Updike. Used by permission of Alfred A. Knopf, an imprint of the Knopf Doubleday Publishing Group, a division of Penguin Random House LLC. All rights reserved. Extracts reproduced by permission of Penguin Books Ltd.

50 James Baldwin, *Giovanni's Room*, in *Early Novels and Short Stories* (New York: Library of America, 1998), p. 223.

51 James Baldwin, *Just Above My Head* (London: Penguin, 1994), p. 564.

52 Baldwin, *Just Above My Head*, pp. 561, 564.

53 Baldwin, *Just Above My Head*, p. 564.

54 James Baldwin, 'Letters to a Journey', in *The Cross of Redemption: Uncollected Writings*, edited and introduced by Randall Kenan (New York: Pantheon Books, 2010), p. 191.

55 For example, Baldwin, 'Letters to a Journey', p. 191.

56 Baldwin, 'Letters to a Journey', p. 195.

57 Baldwin, 'Letters to a Journey', p. 195.

58 'It's Hard To Be James Baldwin' (interview with Herbert R. Lottman, 1972), in *Conversations with James Baldwin*, p. 111.

59 James Baldwin, 'Incident in London', in *Magpie* (1941), Beinecke Rare Book and Manuscript Library, https://collections.library.yale.edu/catalog/17400877 (accessed 28 May 2024).

60 Baldwin, 'Incident in London'.

61 James Baldwin, 'Stranger in the Village', in *Collected Essays*, p. 129.

62 David Leeming, *James Baldwin: A Biography* (New York: Arcade Publishing, 2015), p. 69.

63 'A Very British Welcome', *Observer*, 28 May 1967, p. 30.

64 Baldwin, *No Name in the Street*, p. 376.

65 Paul Gilroy, 'Interview with James Baldwin', *City Limits*, 15–21 March 1985, p. 73.

66 'If This Man Didn't Exist He'd Have To Be Invented', *Daily Mail*, 22 February 1965, p. 8.

67 Baldwin, *No Name in the Street*, p. 407.

68 'Civil Rights': James Baldwin interview, *Mavis on Four* (1987).

69 James Baldwin, 'Notes for *The Amen Corner*', in *The Amen Corner* (New York: Dial Press, 1968), p. xv.

70 Baldwin, 'Notes for *The Amen Corner*', p. xv.

Chapter 4: Mistakes, we'd made a few, too many to mention

1 James Baldwin, 'As Much Truth As One Can Bear', in *The Cross of Redemption: Uncollected Writings*, edited and introduced by Randall Kenan (New York: Pantheon Books, 2010), p. 28.

2 'James Baldwin: 'How to Cool It', *Esquire*, July 1968, https://www.esquire.com/news-politics/a23960/james-baldwin-cool-it (accessed 29 May 2024).

3 Cited by David Leeming, 'The White Problem' (8 January 2007), *Pen America*: https://pen.org/the-white-problem (accessed 29 May 2024).

4 James Baldwin, 'The White Man's Guilt', in *Collected Essays*, edited by Toni Morrison (New York: The Library of America, 1998), p. 723.

5 James Baldwin, 'Everybody's Protest Novel', in *Collected Essays*, p. 14.

6 James Baldwin, *Go Tell It on the Mountain* (London: Penguin, 1991), p. 57.

7 Baldwin, *Go Tell It on the Mountain*, p. 58.

8 Baldwin, *Go Tell It on the Mountain*, p. 17.

9 Baldwin, *Go Tell It on the Mountain*, p. 19.

10 Baldwin, *Go Tell It on the Mountain*, p. 16.

11 James Baldwin, *Just Above My Head* (London: Penguin, 1994), p. 589.

12 James Baldwin, *The Fire Next Time*, in *Collected Essays*, p. 312.

13 James Baldwin, 'To Crush the Serpent', in *The Cross of Redemption*, p. 161.

14 James Baldwin and Nikki Giovanni, *A Dialogue*, foreword by Ida Lewis, afterword by Orde Coombs (Philadelphia: J. B. Lippincott, 1973), p. 38.

15 Felicia Lee, 'Trying to Bring Baldwin's Complex Voice Back to the Classroom', *New York Times*, 14 April 2014, https://www.nytimes.com/2014/04/25/books/james-baldwin-born-90-years-ago-is-fading-in-classrooms.html (accessed 29 May 2024).

16 Melanie Walsh, 'Tweets of a Native Son' (2023), https://tweetsofanativeson.com/BlackLivesMatter-Baldwin (accessed 29 May 2024).

17 'A Letter on Justice and Open Debate', *Harper's Magazine* (7 July 2020), https://harpers.org/a-letter-on-justice-and-open-debate (accessed 29 May 2024).

18 See Walsh, 'Tweets of a Native Son'.

19 Thomas Chatterton Williams, *X* (Twitter), 9 June 2020, https://twitter.com/thomaschattwill/status/1270444628752375809 (accessed 29 May 2024).

20 Benin Bryant, 'The Lovers' Quarrel Between Free Speech and Cancel Culture', *Medium*, 28 July 2020, https://beninbf.medium.com/a-lovers-quarrel-between-free-speech-and-cancel-culture (accessed 29 May 2024).

21 James Baldwin 'Everybody's Protest Novel', in *Collected Essays*, p. 12.

22 Baldwin, 'Everybody's Protest Novel', p. 15.

23 Baldwin 'Everybody's Protest Novel', p. 17.

24 Baldwin 'Everybody's Protest Novel', p. 13.

25 Nick Cave, 'What Is Mercy for You?', *The Red Hand Files*, August 2020, https://www.theredhandfiles.com/what-is-mercy-for-you (accessed 20 May 2024).

26 Norman Mailer, *Advertisements for Myself* (Cambridge, MA: Harvard University Press, 1992), p. 417.

27 Mailer, *Advertisements for Myself*, p. 472.

28 James Baldwin, 'The Black Boy Looks at the White Boy', in *Collected Essays*, p. 272.

29 All references to 'The White Negro' relate to the online version of the original 1957 *Dissent* article, https://www.dissentmagazine.org/online_articles/the-white-negro-fall-1957 (accessed 29 May 2024).

30 LeRoi Jones, 'The Myth of a "Negro" Literature', in *Within the Circle: An Anthology of African American Literary Criticism from*

the Harlem Renaissance to the Present, edited by Angelyn Mitchell (Durham: Duke University Press, 1994), p. 171.

31 Langston Hughes, *The Big Sea* (New York: Hill & Wang, 1993), p. 228.

32 'Howl', by Allen Ginsberg. Copyright © 1956, 2010, Allen Ginsberg LLC., used by permission of The Wylie Agency (UK) Limited. See https://www.poetryfoundation.org/poems/49303/howl (accessed 29 May 2024).

33 Baldwin, 'The Black Boy Looks at the White Boy', p. 278.

34 Baldwin, 'The Black Boy Looks at the White Boy', p. 278.

35 James Baldwin, 'If Black English Isn't a Language, Then Tell Me, What Is?', in *Collected Essays*, p. 781.

36 James Baldwin, 'Sermons and Blues', in *Collected Essays*, p. 615.

37 Vilém Flusser, *On Doubt*, edited by Siegfried Zielinski, translated by Rodrigo Maltez Novaes (Minneapolis: Univocal Publishing, 2014), p. 3.

38 Jack Kerouac, prefatory note, in *Mexico City Blues* (New York: Grove Press, 1959), no pagination; James Baldwin, '"What's the Reason Why? A Symposium by Best-Selling Authors": James Baldwin on *Another Country*', in *The Cross of Redemption: Uncollected Writings*, edited and introduced by Randall Kenan (New York: Pantheon, 2010), p. 40.

39 Jack Kerouac, 'Notes of 1950 February', in *The Unknown Kerouac: Rare, Unpublished and Newly Translated Writings*, edited by Todd Tietchen, translated by Christophe Cloutier (New York: Library of America, 2016), p. 58. 'The Price of the Ticket' is the title of an essay that was used as the introduction to Baldwin's volume of essays *The Price of the Ticket: Collected Nonfiction, 1948–1985* (New York: St Martin's Press, 1985).

40 Elsa Knight Thompson and John Leonard, 'A Conversation with James Baldwin', first broadcast on 6 June 1963, KPFA radio, Berkeley, California, transcription at https://americanarchive.org/catalog28-8s4jm23q52 (accessed 29 May 2024).

41 Kenneth Rexroth, 'Jazz Poetry', https://www.bopsecrets.org/rexroth/essays/jazz-poetry.htm (accessed 29 May 2024).

42 James Campbell, *Talking at the Gates: A Life of James Baldwin* (London: Faber & Faber, 1991), p. 143.

43 David Leeming, *James Baldwin: A Biography* (New York: Alfred A. Knopf, 1994), p. 185.

44 Campbell, *Talking at the Gates*, p. 157.

45 William Styron, 'This Quiet Dust', *Harper's Magazine*, April 1965, p. 145.

46 William Styron, *The Confessions of Nat Turner* (London: Picador, 1994), p. ix.

47 Sam Tanenhaus, 'The Literary Battle for Nat Turner's Legacy', *Vanity Fair*, 3 August 2016, https://www.vanityfair.com/culture/2016/08/the-literary-battle-for-nat-turners-legacy (accessed 29 May 2024).

48 *William Styron's Nat Turner: Ten Black Writers Respond*, edited by John Henrik Clarke (Boston: Beacon Press, 1968), p. viii.

49 Lerone Bennett Jr., 'Nat's Last White Man', in *William Styron's Nat Turner*, p. 5.

50 Michael Thelwell, 'Back With the Wind: Mr. Styron and the Reverend Turner', in *William Styron's Nat Turner*, p. 80.

51 Julius Lester, 'James Baldwin – Reflections of a Maverick', in *Conversations with James Baldwin*, edited by Fred R. Standley and Louis H. Pratt (Jackson: University Press of Mississippi, 1989), p. 229.

52 James Baldwin, 'Introduction', in *Duties, Pleasures and Conflicts: Essays in Struggle*, by Michael Thelwell (Amherst: University of Massachusetts Press, 1987), p. xxi.

53 Ella Creamer, 'Salman Rushdie: Allow Writers to Create Characters Outside of Their Own Experience', *Guardian*, 23 October 2023, https://www.theguardian.com/books/2023/oct/23/salman-rushdie-allow-writers-to-create-characters-outside-of-their-own-experience (accessed 29 May 2024).

54 Baldwin and Giovanni, *A Dialogue*, p. 45; James Baldwin, 'Color', in *Collected Essays*, p. 676.

55 Tanenhaus, 'The Literary Battle for Nat Turner's Legacy'.

56 Henry Louis Gates Jr., '"Authenticity" or the Lesson of Little Tree', *New York Times Book Review*, 24 November 1991, p. 26.

57 Cited by Hoyt W. Fuller, 'Towards a Black Aesthetic', in *The Black Aesthetic*, edited by Gayle Addison Jr. (New York: Doubleday & Company, 1971), p. 4; Irving Howe, 'Black Boys and Native Sons', in *Selected Writings, 1950–1990* (San Diego: Harcourt Brace Jovanovich, 1990), p. 129.

58 Colin MacInnes, 'Dark Angel: The Writings of James Baldwin', *Encounter*, no. 21 (July–December 1963), p. 26.

59 W. J. Weatherby, *Squaring Off: Mailer v. Baldwin* (London: Robson Books, 1977), p. 7.

60 Gates, '"Authenticity"', pp. 28, 29.

61 Don L. Lee, 'Towards a Definition: Black Poetry of the Sixties', in *The Black Aesthetic*, pp. 227–8.

62 Gates, '"Authenticity"', p. 1.

63 Yvonne Neverson, 'The Artist Has Always Been a Disturber of the Peace', in *Conversations with James Baldwin*, p. 171.

64 Franklin Foer, 'Megan Rapinoe Answers the Critics', *The Atlantic*, 22 August 2023, https://www.theatlantic.com/culture/archive/2023/08/

megan-rapinoe-retirement-womens-world-cup-interview/675073 (accessed 29 May 2024).

65 James Baldwin, 'Autobiographical Notes', in *Collected Essays*, p. 18.

66 Baldwin, 'As Much Truth As One Can Bear', p. 33.

67 Philip Larkin, 'Vers de Société', in *Collected Poems* (London: Marvell Press and Faber & Faber, 1988), p. 181. © Philip Larkin and reprinted by permission of Faber & Faber Ltd.

68 Robert Brustein, 'Everybody Knows My Name' (review of James Baldwin and Richard Avedon, *Nothing Personal*), *New York Review of Books*, 17 December 1964, https://www.nybooks.com/articles/1964/12/17/everybody-knows-my-name (accessed 29 May 2024).

69 Brustein, 'Everybody Knows My Name'.

70 Brustein, 'Everybody Knows My Name'.

71 Irving Howe, 'Black Boys and Native Sons', p. 121; Harold Cruse, *The Crisis of the Negro Intellectual: A Historical Analysis of the Failure of Black Leadership* (1967; reprint, with a foreword by Bazel E. Allen and Ernest J. Wilson III, New York: Quill, 1984), p. 200; Albert Murray, *The Omni-Americans: New Perspectives on Black Experience and American Culture* (New York: Outerbridge & Dienstfrey, 1970), p. 148.

72 Baldwin's heavily redacted FBI files can be accessed online, gratis, at https://vault.fbi.gov/james-baldwin (accessed 29 May 2024).

73 Philip Roth, 'Channel X: Two Plays on the Race Conflict', *New York Review*, 28 May 1964, https://www.nybooks.com/articles/1964/05/28/channel-x-two-plays-on-the-race-conflict (accessed 29 May 2024).

74 Mario Puzo, 'His Cardboard Lovers', *New York Times Book Review*, 23 June 1968, p. 5.

75 Eliot Fremont Smith, 'Books of the Times: Another Track', *New York Times*, 31 May 1968, p. 27.

76 Eugenia Collier, 'The Phrase Unbearably Repeated', *Phylon*, vol. 25, no. 3 (1964), p. 288.

77 Augusta Strong, review of James Baldwin, *Another Country*, in *Freedomways*, vol. 2, no. 4 (fall 1962), p. 501.

78 Baldwin and Giovanni, *A Dialogue*, pp. 52, 55.

79 James Baldwin, *Tell Me How Long the Train's Been Gone* (London: Penguin, 1994), pp. 291, 316.

80 James Baldwin, 'The Harlem Ghetto', in *Collected Essays*, p. 53.

81 Baldwin quoted by David Leeming, 'The White Problem', *PEN America: A Journal for Writers and Readers*, no. 2 (fall 2001) and Baldwin in Margaret Mead and James Baldwin, *A Rap on Race* (New York: Dell, 1971), p. 136.

Epilogue: Thou poor ghost

1   *World Alzheimer Report 2019: Attitudes to Dementia*, https://www.alzint.org/u/WorldAlzheimerReport2019.pdf (accessed 29 May 2024).

2   See the Dementia Statistics Hub, Alzheimer's Research UK, https://dementiastatistics.org/about-dementia/diagnosis (accessed 29 May 2024). See also Anna Bawden, 'Inequality Leaving 115,000 Dementia Cases "Undiagnosed" in England', *Guardian*, 23 October 2023, https://www.theguardian.com/society/2023/oct/23/inequality-leaving-115000-dementia-cases-undiagnosed-in-england (accessed 29 May 2024).

3   Stefan Merrill Block, 'A Place Beyond Words: A Literature of Alzheimer's', *New Yorker*, 20 August 2014, https://www.newyorker.com/books/page-turner/place-beyond-words-literature-alzheimers (accessed 29 May 2024).

4   Lynne Malcolm and Olivia Willis, '"Still Alice" and Explaining Neuroscience Through Fiction', https://www.abc.net.au/listen/programs/allinthemind/lisa-genova-still-alice-alzheimers-huntingtons/7218532 (accessed 29 May 2024).

5   Pieter Vermeulen, 'Homo Sacer/Homo Demens. The Epistemology of Dementia in Contemporary Literature and Theory', in *The Politics of Dementia: Forgetting and Remembering the Violent Past in Literature, Film and Graphic Narratives*, edited by Irmela Marei Krüger-Fürhoff, Nina Schmidt and Sue Vice (Berlin, Boston: De Gruyter, 2022), p. 41.

6   William S. Burroughs, *The Western Lands* (London: Picador, 1987), p. 258.

Further reading

James Baldwin's writings

Five of James Baldwin's volumes of essays – *Notes of a Native Son* (1955), *Nobody Knows My Name* (1961), *The Fire Next Time* (1963), *No Name in the Street* (1972) and *The Devil Finds Work* (1976) – can be found in the *Collected Essays*, edited by Toni Morrison (Library of America, 1998), as well as thirty-six other essays and a chronology of his life and work. The volume does not include his last work of non-fiction, *The Evidence of Things Not Seen* (1985).

Another anthology of James Baldwin's writings appeared during his lifetime: *The Price of the Ticket: Collected Nonfiction, 1948–1985* (New York: St Martin's Press/Marek, 1985). This volume of fifty-two essays has some notable omissions, including 'Preservation of Innocence', in which Baldwin discusses homosexuality. The essay was first published in *Zero* (summer 1949) and was not reprinted in *The Price of the Ticket*. It was finally published in the *Collected Essays*. *The Cross of Redemption: Uncollected Writings*, edited and introduced by Randall Kenan (Pantheon Books, 2010) contains previously uncollected essays, a short story, public letters, forewords and afterwords to books, and Baldwin's reviews published between 1947 and 1985.

Baldwin's six novels – *Go Tell It on the Mountain* (1953), *Giovanni's Room* (1956), *Another Country* (1962), *Tell Me How Long the Train's Been Gone* (1968), *If Beale Street Could Talk* (1974) and *Just Above My Head* (1979) – are all in print and are widely available. His only collection of short stories, *Going to Meet the Man* (1965), includes his most famous one, 'Sonny's Blues'.

Baldwin's first play, *The Amen Corner*, was performed at Howard University, Washington, DC, in 1955; it was not published in its entirety until 1968. His second play, *Blues for Mister Charlie*, was published in 1964, the year that it was performed on Broadway. There are also four known versions of the unfinished play *The Welcome Table*, which was written during the 1970s. That play has not been published.

Baldwin wrote two collections of poetry, only one of which, *Jimmy's Blues: Selected Poems*, has been published (Michael Joseph, 1983). A second collection, *Gypsy & Other Poems*, was limited to a print run of 325 copies (Gehenna Press, 1989).

Baldwin gave scores of interviews during his lifetime, some of which have been collected in *Conversations with James Baldwin*, edited by Fred R. Standley and Louis H. Pratt (University Press of Mississippi, 1989). Baldwin's conversation with the anthropologist Margaret Mead was published as *A Rap on Race* (Dell, 1971). In 1971, Baldwin was filmed with the poet Nikki Giovanni for the PBS television series *SOUL!* The transcript was published as *A Dialogue* (J. B. Lippincott, 1973).

Baldwin on film

Baldwin was an electrifying speaker and there is a lot of footage of him on YouTube. There are also a handful of films about him, some of which are not well known:

Un étranger dans le village (1962), directed by Pierre Koralnik (29 mins). Baldwin revisits the small Swiss village where he finished his first novel, and he reads his essay 'Stranger in the Village' in French.

Take This Hammer (1964), directed by Richard O. Moore (45 mins). Baldwin visits San Francisco in 1963, where he speaks to members of the African American community.

Baldwin vs. Buckley (1965), directed by John McGonagle (59 mins). Filmed for the BBC, the film captures Baldwin debating with William F. Buckley Jr. at the University of Cambridge in 1965, where the motion was 'Has the American Dream Been Achieved at the Expense of the American Negro?'

Baldwin's Nigger (1969), directed by Horace Ové (46 mins). The late Sir Horace Ové filmed Baldwin giving a talk to West Indian students in London, along with the comedian and activist Dick Gregory.

James Baldwin: From Another Place (1970), directed by Sedat Pakay (12 mins). Filmed during May 1970 in Istanbul, where Baldwin was living, this intimate portrait gives insight into Baldwin's thoughts on America and Turkey.

Meeting the Man: James Baldwin in Paris (1970), directed by Terence Dixon (26 mins). This is a short and terse documentary about white filmmakers who are no match for Baldwin's brilliance.

I Heard It Through the Grapevine (1982), directed by Dick Fontaine and Pat Hartley (95 mins). Recently restored, this documentary follows Baldwin during the early 1980s as he reflects on the Civil Rights Movement twenty years earlier.

James Baldwin: The Price of the Ticket (1989), directed by Karen Thorsen (87 mins). This documentary, which opens with a moving scene of Baldwin's funeral, contains some compelling footage of Baldwin and those who knew him.

I Am Not Your Negro (2016), directed by Raoul Peck (93 mins). Narrated by Samuel L. Jackson, using only Baldwin's words, this Oscar-nominated and BAFTA Award-winning documentary brought Baldwin to new audiences. The film is based around a book he had barely begun, *Remember This House*, intended to be an account of three Civil Rights leaders – Malcolm X, Martin Luther King Jr. and Medgar Evers – but the voiceover in fact reads from over a dozen disparate texts by Baldwin.

Works on Baldwin

There are a number of biographies of Baldwin. The two most informative are James Campbell's *Talking at the Gates: A Life of James Baldwin*, originally published in 1991 by Faber & Faber and revised and updated in 2021 by Polygon; and David Leeming's *James Baldwin: A Biography*, originally published by Alfred A. Knopf in 1994 and available in subsequent editions.

Since the new millennium – and especially in the last decade – there have been scores of books and articles on Baldwin, most by academics. Among the most notable is Eddie Glaude Jr.'s bestselling book *Begin Again: James Baldwin's America and Its Urgent Lessons for Today* (Vintage, 2022).

James Baldwin Review is an annual journal dedicated to the life and work of the writer. It is open access (i.e., free) and is written with the general reader in mind, as well as academics.

Websites about Alzheimer's

Alzheimer's Society: https://www.alzheimers.org.uk/
Alzheimer's Research UK: https://dementiastatistics.org/
Alzheimer's Association (USA): https://www.alz.org/

Selected books about memory and Alzheimer's

Alkon, Daniel L., *Memory's Voice: Deciphering the Mind–Brain Code* (Perennial, 1994).
Comer, Meryl, *Slow Dancing with a Stranger: Lost and Found in the Age of Alzheimer's* (HarperOne, 2015).
DeBaggio, Thomas, *Losing My Mind: An Intimate Look at Life with Alzheimer's* (Free Press, 2002).
Genova, Lisa, *Remember: The Science of Memory and the Art of Forgetting* (Allen & Unwin, 2022).
Harper, Lynn Casteel, *On Vanishing: Mortality, Dementia, and What It Means to Disappear* (Catapult, 2020).
Jebelli, Joseph, *In Pursuit of Memory: The Fight Against Alzheimer's* (John Murray, 2018).
Mitchell, Wendy, *What I Wish People Knew About Dementia: From Someone Who Knows* (Bloomsbury, 2023).

Quiroga, Rodrigo Quian, *The Forgetting Machine: Memory, Perception, and the 'Jennifer Aniston Neuron'* (BenBella Books, 2017).

Shaw, Julia, *The Memory Illusion: Remembering, Forgetting, and the Science of False Memory* (Random House, 2017).

Shenk, David, *The Forgetting*, with a preface by Adam Phillips (Flamingo, 2003).

Selected novels, memoirs and stories about dementia

'Dementia Fiction', a Queen's University Belfast blog, 'investigates how the language of contemporary fiction represents the minds of characters with dementia': https://blogs.qub.ac.uk/dementiafiction. Jan Carson and Jane Lugea have co-edited a collection of commissioned short stories involving those living with dementia, *A Little Unsteadily into Light* (New Island Books, 2022).

Bayley, John, *Elegy for Iris* (St Martin's Press, 1999). Memoir.

Crossan, Sarah, *Toffee* (Bloomsbury YA, 2016). Young adult.

Dean, Deborah, *The Madonnas of Leningrad* (William Morrow & Co., 2006). Novel.

Doshi, Avni, *Burnt Sugar* (Penguin, 2021). Novel.

Downham, Jenny, *Unbecoming* (David Fickling Books, 2016). Young adult.

Ernaux, Annie, *I Remain in Darkness*, translated by Tanya Leslie (Fitzcarraldo Editions, 2019). Memoir.

Healey, Emma, *Elizabeth Is Missing* (Penguin, 2015). Novel.

Hepworth, Sally, *The Things We Keep* (Pan, 2016). Novel.

McKervey, Henrietta, *The Heart of Everything* (Hachette, 2017). Novel.

McKnight, Harriet, *Rain Birds* (Black Inc., 2018). Novel.

Roca, Paco, *Wrinkles* (Knockabout, 2015). Graphic novel.
Self, Will, *Phone* (Penguin, 2018). Novel.
Smith, Ali, *There but for the* (Penguin, 2012). Novel.
Verhulst, Dimitri, *The Latecomer*, translated by David Colmer
    (Portobello Books, 2016). Novel.

Index

Index

EU authorised representative for GPSR:
Easy Access System Europe, Mustamäe tee 50,
10621 Tallinn, Estonia
gpsr.requests@easproject.com